The Buena Salud® Guide to

UNDERSTANDING DEPRESSION

AND

ENJOYING LIFE

JANE L. DELGADO, PHD, MS

Carmen —
Con mucho
cariño y un
abrazo fuerte,

Buena
Salud
Press

This book is published in the United States of America
First Edition
ISBN: 978-0-9979954-2-8
1 2 3 4 5 6 7 8 9 10

Library of Congress Control Number: 2020941684

This book is designed to provide accurate and authoritative information in regard to the subject matter covered. It is not intended to substitute for medical advice from a qualified health professional. The reader should consult his or her medical, health, or other competent professional before adopting any of the suggestions in this book or drawing inferences from it.

The author and the publisher specifically disclaim all responsibility for any liability, loss, or risk, personal or otherwise, that is incurred as a consequence, directly or indirectly, of the use and application of any of the contents of this book.

CONTENTS

FOREWORD

For the past 40 years I have worked to reach all communities with the message that mental health and mental wellness need our nation's attention and that mental illnesses can be treated and managed. In her book, The *Buena Salud*® Guide to Understanding Depression and Enjoying Life, Dr. Jane Delgado inspires us with the stories of men and women who have experienced depression, provides advice we can use for treating and managing it, and challenges all of us to end the stigma associated with this serious disorder

It frustrates—and motivates—me to know that the major stumbling block to treatment is still stigma, something I and other advocates have worked for decades to overcome. Too often stigma comes from distortions that we see in the media about depression and other mental illnesses. We need voices of compassion like Dr. Delgado's that provide accurate, practical information such as that contained in this valuable guide.

I have heard from people across the country about all they have done to recover from their depression. But, sadly, many initially were reluctant to seek help. Some did not know that help was available, and others felt uncomfortable seeking help, even when it was accessible. If you or a loved one is depressed, please get the help you need. The *Su Familia* National Hispanic Family Health Helpline at 1-866-SU-FAMILIA (1-866-783-2645), available in Spanish and English, is just one of the many wonderful and trusted resources that Dr. Delgado recommends for identifying free or low-cost mental health services where you live.

Drawing from her experience as a clinician and health advocate, Dr. Delgado provides a concise guide to what you need to know about depression in its many forms and answers the most common questions Hispanics ask about depression. She gives the reader the best online sources for information, a guide for selecting a mental health professional, and, the most recent advances in telehealth.

I am proud to have worked in partnership with Dr. Delgado, one of this nation's most trusted health leaders, since my time as First Lady and then as part of the Carter Center Mental Health Program. I applaud her work in The *Buena Salud®* Guide to Understanding Depression and Enjoying Life and am confident that readers will find hope and a path for recovery and wellness.

Rosalynn Carter
Former First Lady and Founder of The Carter Center Mental Health Program

INTRODUCTION

Every book in the *Buena Salud®* series was written with the
intent of bringing the most up-to-date, commercial-free,
and reliable information to you. As with all of the books in
this series, my intention is to update you whenever significant
advances are made in our understanding of each condition. The
urgency to update this book was different: it was driven by the
impact of COVID-19 both during and after the crisis.

During the initial crisis, a fortunate few were able to work
from home and were happy to do so; others experienced
increased financial worries and anxiety since they had lost
their sole source of income. Some suffered lost opportunities
that could never be replaced, such as witnessing the birth of a
child, achieving their dream of a small business, or expanding
their career. Moreover, countless deaths could not be mourned
through burial rituals, which often provide some comfort to
survivors. Our sadness was palpable, like a fine mist that clouded
our vision. A person had to be aware of their feelings so as to not
to be overwhelmed and spiral into their first major depression.
Those who knew depression well had to take cautious steps

to avoid finding themselves slipping into its grips. This was a challenging task for all.

The mandate to stay home was not always welcomed. Some were happy to not commute and welcomed the freedom of working from home. For others, this mandate highlighted the fact that home was not a place to be in for extended periods: to them, their home served as a place to sleep in but not to live in. Staying home brought other issues to the forefront.

Saying "home is where the heart is" turned out to be a cliché from another time. Home was not always the happiest or most nurturing place. Home was not a safe place for everyone, as the rate of most crimes decreased but for the notable exception of domestic violence. Calls for assistance increased during quarantine as numerous people found themselves locked inside with an angry, potentially violent partner. For them, this was an incredibly complicated time.

New relationships that had already been tenuous were unravelling as a result of extensive separation and mandatory distance, while older relationships, which had thrived on each person having their own individual space, suffered as a result of their forced 24/7 togetherness. And the scores of religious institutions that provided spiritual nurturance for people were closed.

At the Alliance, we did what we could to support as many people as possible. The Su Familia helpline was available for callers, and we provided information on what to do to protect ourselves and our loved ones. But we were concerned about what would happen afterwards.

Life had changed along many dimensions.

Both our collective and individual senses of how we work had experienced a major shift. It was clear that the ability to work from home was now feasible for about one third of all workers. Employers realized that having people work from home would not hurt their bottom line, and in some cases, would actually help them save money. People who had been working towards a career saw their industry shattered as many people, forced to stay home, could no longer return to their job because it no longer existed. Others, who had championed their independence by being self-employed at the frontline of the gig economy, found that their gigs had disappeared. A survey conducted during COVID-19 reported that depressive symptoms were not only high, but that more than 25 percent of the sample reported moderate to severe anxiety symptoms.[1] For most people, especially essential workers, working from home was not an option. It was clear that the immediate period post-quarantine was just the beginning of what would be an ongoing process of adjustments.

The feelings that people continue to experience are very real—apprehension, dread, instability, loneliness, desperation. This is not surprising. Research on the aftereffects of natural or manmade disasters document long term negative impacts on a person's mental status.[2] Whether it was 9/11, Hurricane María, Deepwater Horizon oil spill, or some other catastrophic event, each one drastically changed those who were impacted. These events made countless people suddenly feel defenseless, increasing their vulnerability to their own psychological challenges.

COVID-19 did more than just impact each one of us: it changed our country and the world. Pandemics bring to the forefront our connectedness to each other globally. People who had had, at best, a limited interest in foreign affairs closely watched the trajectory of illness, death, and recovery closely as the virus traveled from one country to another. We compared ourselves to other countries where no other previous comparisons had been made. We felt both at one with the world and a strong desire to stay home. This was most obvious in our sudden unwillingness to fly on planes or travel to exotic places. These previous common activities quickly diminished or disappeared altogether. How people thought about foreign travel was no longer the same. The veneer of safety, coupled with the belief that one would be able to readily return home, was shattered. One man mentioned that, before the COVID-19 outbreak, he had been ridiculed for limiting his travel to places where, if anything bad happened, he would be able to walk home…even if he had to walk for thousands of miles. After the pandemic, few were making fun of him, and he felt vindicated for narrowing his travel in that way.

We also had the health imperative to engage in social distancing. This essential practice is the opposite of our human need for intimacy, closeness, and touch. Decades ago, Harry Harlow's research with infant rhesus monkeys provided compelling evidence that infants need love and comfort; now we know that that need is true for humans throughout their lives. The biological push for social contact is driven by the chemicals in our brain.[3] It is not surprising that there is plenty of evidence that loneliness and feelings of isolation can also be deadly. We continue to be concerned about the long-term impact on all of us in how we interact with each other. Anxiety and sadness is still prevalent as we attempt to figure out how best to function in this new environment. Life had changed quickly, and while there were many disruptions, there were some new paths that we could take.

Since the same old ways of doing things were no longer possible, we had to recalibrate our expectations and our own behaviors. Suddenly we witnessed a pervasive acceptance of telehealth, from coverage by insurance companies, which had previously been reluctant to cover such visits, to health care providers and their practices embracing the virtual health visits that they had previously disparaged.

Mental health providers had to find a way to marry the flexibility and opportunities provided by virtual therapy to a treatment plan that relied on building a therapeutic alliance, as well as enhancing and healing people's connectedness to others. Psychological practices needed to be significantly retooled in order to improve the mental health of people and communities.

There were numerous heroes who rose to the occasion, from health care providers to people who took public transportation to get to an essential job that they had never thought of as essential before the pandemic. Some people were fine throughout the crisis: one person wrote me and said, "This quiet time was a blessing." However, that was not everybody's experience. We were not all in this together, and some suffered much more than others. There were also people who dealt with some degree of depression before, during, and after the crisis. This book is updated for them: I want to provide them with tools that have been modified to address our new way of life.

The first edition of this book was about overcoming depression. While the word "overcoming" may make it sound like a positive goal, it may not be possible for everybody. In fact, setting up "overcoming" depression as the goal may be unrealistic and can actually make a person more depressed if they feel they are going down the very path that they are trying to avoid. There is a huge range of symptoms included when someone says, "I am depressed," and we must understand what it means when we say or someone we know says those words.

Certainly, there is no single known event or factor that will always produce the same feeling in every person. Death, divorce, or loss may have a major impact on one person and yet have little or no effect on another. One person may suffer a major loss and be sad for a long time, while another person experiencing the same kind of loss may use it as motivation to push themselves toward a new trajectory. Moreover, the word "depression" in our daily conversation has a different meaning for each person. When someone is diagnosed with clinical depression or its more persistent forms, they require understanding, knowledge, and concrete action. There is a wide range of options for what a person can and should do to manage their depression.

Most of us have to accept that our feelings are real and not discount them. At the same time, we have to throw out myths that immobilize or hurt us. Thoughts and feelings may make a person feel bad and prevent the enjoyment of certain activities that were previously enjoyed. While we are all familiar with having not-so-good feelings, too many of us tend to believe that, in every instance, we should be able to make those feelings just go away. We often believe that we should be able to shake it off and keep going. And while this may be true in some cases, some of us may need additional help to regain our ability to enjoy life.

But the ways in which we feel and experience life are also greatly affected by how our brains, microbiomes, and bodies function. The biological basis of depression is not an excuse for bad behavior; instead, it is a way to understand that the chemistry in our gut and brain are connected to what we feel and experience. So far there is no gene test, blood test, or brain scan that can tell us definitively that someone is or is at risk of becoming depressed, nor is there a way to predict what is the best intervention.

We all go through feeling sad or down at some point in life— some of us more often than others. Sadness is a natural reaction to situations that cause pain or are upsetting. Depression is different from sadness. If you are the one who is depressed, then you need to know that there is no reason for you to spend your life being anxious or miserable. Likewise, if someone close to you is depressed, there are steps you can take to better support them to seek help without draining your own emotional and physical reserves in the process.

Depression is neither a way of life nor something that just has to be endured. There is much that can be done to get to a better place. Far too many people have endured depression rather than moving away from it. None of us should spend our lives suffering, and that is why this book is so important. Life can get much better if we take the steps that we need to take and seek treatment for depression.

It is amazing that people are still reluctant to seek help. It is true that more celebrities are talking about dealing with their mental health issues, such as J. Balvin, Selena Gomez, Michael Phelps, and many more. For most people, though, seeking help is still tough for many reasons. Some have concerns about how others will perceive them. Others don't seek help because of their own discomfort with their thoughts and feelings. And many still have misconceptions about treatments, therapies, and medications. Moreover, plenty of people may not know what tools and resources they need and can access.

This book addresses these topics in several concrete ways. The first goal is to make sure that it is clear what is meant by depression. While we use the word in our everyday conversations, it can have different implications depending on how it presents itself. Both biological factors and environmental factors play a critical role in depression. This is why understanding the influence of your genes, your brain, and the balance of hormones and microbes is essential. Similarly, your feelings, emotions, and self-esteem are powerful levers in controlling depression. All of these factors can contribute to depression. Without doubt it is a condition that has an impact on the body, mind, and spirit.

The second goal is to clearly present options for you to consider. You can take many actions on your own, and you may already know most of them. But knowing and doing are very different. This book includes and explains three simple self-statements to encourage you along your path to a healthier life and make it easier for you to manage depression. Once you incorporate these statements into your life, you will be in a better place.

When you cannot seem to do it on your own, you need to seek help. Getting help is an important step, and to help you, this book includes a description of different types of mental health professionals. There are also many treatment options. You'll find a lot of information about treatment in the media (that is, in social media, advertisements, newspapers, magazines, radio, TV, and the internet), but much of it is designed to have you buy a product or service, and many are clickbait that, at best, are alarming rather than informative. In this book, I have curated the facts on some of the most cutting-edge topics regarding the treatment of depression, including light therapy, while providing you with the latest findings about areas in which we still have unanswered questions, such as brain stimulation therapy. Working with a mental health professional will help you to sort through the options that are best for you.

The last part of this book provides key resources: non-commercial websites, crisis helplines, descriptions of the different types of mental health professionals, suggestions on how to select a mental health provider, and telehealth resources.

The information in this book is provided with the intention of making life better for everyone—those with depression, those we love who have depression, and those of us who have to address the consequences of untreated depression. Once you understand that there are options for depression, you can take the necessary steps you need to manage it. Remember that if you apply the lessons learned by others and shared in this book, as well as the findings from science that are presented here, you will be able to more fully understand depression and consequently improve your life.

There is no reason to suffer in silence. Do what you can on your own and seek professional support as needed. Be certain that with time, you will get better.

UNDERSTANDING DEPRESSION

I f you were not feeling well physically, perhaps you would take your temperature. If your temperature was 99°F, you would probably take one set of actions. If it were 103°F, you would probably opt for a more aggressive treatment and take some over-the-counter medicines that you had at home. If after three days you still had a high temperature, you would probably see a health care provider, contact your usual sources for health care advice, and take further steps toward recovery.

What do you do when you are sad? What do you tell others to do? What do you do if the sadness extends from days into weeks? Too often, we respond in the same way: we ignore it, hide it, and do nothing.

We endure our sadness and misery because at some fundamental level, we believe that being sad is part of life. And while that is true, sad moments should not be a constant part of life. It is essential to understand the distinction between simply "feeling blue" and being so sad that it inhibits you from engaging in the activities you normally do and enjoy.

Whether they are sad for a day or two weeks, most people usually try to take care of it themselves. The unspoken assumption is that it is all "in your head" and "there is nothing really wrong with you," so you should just have to get over it.

But something that is in your head is very real and can have long-term consequences that compromise your well-being. You need to understand and address what is going on in your head so that you can sort out whatever is causing your unease. Unfortunately, with respect to mental health, there is still considerable reluctance to acknowledge that someone has a real condition that needs to be taken care of.

CULTURAL MESSAGES

Our society's dominant culture celebrates rugged individualism and tells us that people need to be stoic. For Hispanics, these values are amplified by the stifling vestiges of *aguantando* or *machismo*. These words represent the cultural message that to be respected, you have to accept anything that is happening in your life, even if it is negative. We communicate these ideas to each other in many ways, across all ages and genders.

Latinas are still socialized to *aguantar* (endure) and not discuss the sorrows they are having or reveal if they are despondent. The expected response is simply to handle things, not complain, and just keep going. If you are pregnant, you are supposed to be happy. If you are not happy, then you have to be quiet about it and just go back to doing your work. Rarely do we hear about or admit to the depression among women during and after pregnancy (perinatal and postpartum depression). *Aguantar* means that, even if you are suffering, you do not admit it and you definitely do not seek professional help.

Others resonate to the strands of *machismo* or *marianismo*, which were cultural norms in the past. These norms were somewhat beneficial, since they made people feel responsible for taking care of others. However, they also contributed to the burden that you always had to appear strong and powerful and could never show feelings of sadness, since that would be a sign of weakness. This was confirmed in a 2016 study of 4,426 people from ages 18 to 74 who self-identified as Hispanic from Central American, Cuban, Dominican, Mexican, Puerto Rican, or South American backgrounds. The results revealed that regardless of sex or Hispanic background, specific components of *machismo* (traditional *machismo*) and *marianismo* (family and spiritual pillar) were associated with higher levels of negative emotions, even after taking income and education into account.[4]

People felt devalued if they talked about their feelings and, to maintain the respect of others, did whatever they had to do to block out the feelings associated with depression. For some, the use of alcohol or other substances—legal or otherwise—provided an easy method to conceal their feelings, but in the long run, this approach only created more problems.

This complex combination of cultural values continues to

suppress help-seeking behaviors. This effect is compounded by the legacy of stigma associated with seeking mental health services. Stigma decreases people's desire to talk to family and friends about mental health problems. Stigma also makes it challenging for those people who are receiving treatment to take their antidepressant medications.[5]

Stigma has always been an enormous barrier to mental health, and while its force has been diminished somewhat in recent years, its impact is still present and palpable. Hispanics with mild, moderate, or severe depressive symptoms were the group least likely to have seen a mental health professional when compared to non-Hispanic blacks or non-Hispanic whites with the same level of symptoms.[6]

But this is slowly changing as most people, especially younger generations, are less likely to be held back by such stigma. For example, it is now common for celebrities to talk to the public about how they deal with their mental health issues. This is especially significant since depression has touched many of our lives: we all know someone who is either depressed or has had to care for someone with depression. Some of us know someone who committed suicide. By hearing others' experiences, we become more open to talk about our problems and seek help.

TALKING ABOUT DEPRESSION

For most people, the term depression collects within it a wide array of experiences from being sad or grieving or even having a bad day. In some instances, however, the sadness is considered typical and expected. For example, when you suffer a loss, it is expected that you will feel sadness. In fact, it would be cause for concern if you did not feel sad. If a loved one died and you were not sad, you would be considered insensitive, callous, or even odd. But depression is different than being sad. It is a feeling that is beyond grief and lasts significantly longer (more on this later). But how do you measure it? The challenge in mental health is one of measurement: how do you know what someone else is experiencing?

For most physical health problems, getting an answer is straightforward and involves some objective test or measurement. When you are diagnosed with high blood pressure or diabetes, it is because the readings your health care provider took were too high. Based on those test results, your health care provider will give you medicines to take, recommend changes to make in your lifestyle, and have you monitor your blood sugar level or blood pressure regularly.

For depression, there is no single objective test or measure to determine when a person is depressed or even measure the intensity of their depression. Trying to determine if someone has depression is further complicated because communication is at the core of one's ability to make an accurate diagnosis. There are questions that can be asked and written tests that can be given, but in order to produce an accurate diagnosis, the person must be able to understand the questions posed by the mental health care provider, honestly answer these questions, and feel comfortable doing so. When a person is depressed, it becomes even more difficult for them to find the words to articulate their experience. In tough circumstances, it can be incredibly challenging to express ourselves and accurately explain our feelings. This is another factor that makes detecting depression difficult.

For Hispanics, diagnosis is even more intricate because issues of language and culture are interwoven with how we describe the emotions we feel. The words we use to describe our despair are often muted when we attempt to translate what we experience into English. The dearth of bilingual and bicultural mental health professionals adds to this problem.

Receiving an accurate assessment is further complicated by the fact that the tests that are used have not always been validated in diverse communities. Additionally, the symptoms that are part of depression, such as generalized aches and pains, headaches, stomach problems, and the like may be confused for physical ailments, when in fact the issue is that the person is exhibiting signs of depression.

DEFINING DEPRESSION

Developing a consistent way to provide a meaningful diagnosis is difficult even for experts, many of whom have been working on this issue for decades. Concepts of mental illness, mental well-being, and mental health are hotly debated. For example, in positive psychology, mental health is not just the absence of mental illness but also the presence of positive emotions and traits. In 2004, Dr. Christopher Peterson and Dr. Martin Seligman took a major step in creating a classification system for the character strengths and virtues that are essential to mental wellness.[7]

Nevertheless, in the United States, we rely on the Diagnostic and Statistical Manual of Mental Disorders (DSM) to help us diagnose mental illness. Since its release in 1952, the DSM has been updated several times. These revised versions include DSM-II (1968), DSM-III (1987), DMS-III-R (1987), DSM-IV (1994), DSM-IV-TR (2000), and DSM-5 (2013).

The DSM is updated to incorporate the latest science and treatments. Cultural and social contexts add even more dimensions to the development of criteria for diagnosis. These updates have involved dozens of committees and hundreds of practitioners. The changes and transformations of the DSM are intensely debated and involve not only the inclusion of new categories and frameworks but also the elimination of obsolete categories.

DSM-5 made it clear that depression and a bipolar disorder (formerly manic-depressive illness or manic depression) are different. While both are mood (affective) disorders, they are distinct from one another. Someone who has a bipolar disorder may have episodes of sadness, but that is not what defines a bipolar disorder. Bipolar disorders are now in their own category as a mood disorder that causes unusual shifts in a person's affects, levels of energy, levels of activity, ability to concentrate, and ability to carry out day to day tasks. DMS-5 also added two depressive disorders— disruptive mood dysregulation disorder (diagnosed in children and adolescents) and premenstrual dysphoric disorder (PMDD).[8]

While mental health professionals in the United States use the DSM (which is owned by the American Psychiatric Association and retails for $210), the rest of the world uses the International Classification of Diseases (ICD) published by the World Health Organization (at no charge). The ICD "is the foundation for the identification of health trends and statistics globally, and the international standard for reporting diseases and health conditions. It is the diagnostic classification standard for all clinical and research purposes. The ICD defines the universe of diseases, disorders, injuries and other related health conditions, listed in a comprehensive, hierarchical fashion."[9] Like the DSM, the ICD is also updated on a regular basis.

Given the global use and access to the ICD, DSM-5 was designed to be practically identical to ICD-10 (published in 1990). In the U.S. we continue to use DSM-5 even though ICD-11 was published in 2018.

The 11 broad categories of mental and behavioral disorders as listed in DSM-5 are:

1. Due to known physiological or organic conditions
2. Due to psychoactive substance use
3. Schizophrenia, schizotypal, delusional, and other non-mood psychotic disorders
4. Mood [affective] disorders
5. Anxiety, dissociative, stress-related, somatoform, and other nonpsychotic mental disorders
6. Behavioral syndromes associated with physiological disturbances and physical factors
7. Disorders of adult personality and behavior
8. Intellectual disabilities
9. Pervasive and specific developmental disorders

10. Behavioral and emotional disorders with onset occurring in childhood and adolescence
11. Unspecified mental disorder

All of this may sound like an exercise in semantics, but its ramifications are crucial because the diagnosis that is given is used to determine the most effective treatment options for the person.

Depression is included in the category of mood (affective) disorders. DSM-5 details the different types of depression and provides important guidelines such as how to distinguish between normal grief and major depression.

GRIEF (BEREAVEMENT) AND MAJOR DEPRESSION

I remember how I felt when my mother died. She was so young, only 67, and I still needed her so very much. My first feeling after she died was of excruciating pain in my jaw. I did not know where that came from and I went to see my internist. He told me that the reason my jaw hurt so very much was because, in all probability, for days I had been locking my jaw. He asked me if I was okay and I said yes. I had had to make so many decisions in the last 72 hours to try to keep Mom alive. It was more stressful to me than I had imagined. And then she was dead.

After she died, I could not sleep at night and, much to my surprise, without trying I lost 10 pounds in three weeks. I just could not eat. The thought of food was too much to bear and when I tried to eat I could not swallow; the food seemed to get stuck in my throat.

I did not want to hear music because it stirred my emotions and I could not tolerate that. Even looking at clothes in my favorite color—red—seemed like too much stimulation for my senses. My red sweaters seemed to screech out to me when I saw them. It was too intense to look at them, so I folded them up and put them away.

It was at that moment that I recognized that I had the symptoms of depression and decided that I should see a mental health professional.

When someone has suffered a loss, it can sometimes seem like they are experiencing a major depressive episode. It is difficult to tell the difference between normal grief and the point at which grief has evolved into major depression. In the past, mental health professionals were asked to keep in mind what was called the bereavement exclusion. This meant that a person should not be diagnosed with depression if they had experienced a loss within the past two months. For many practitioners, the two-month exclusion seemed too short and caused considerable debate.

Ultimately, DSM-5 dropped the bereavement exclusion, acknowledging that bereavement could last longer than two months. Moreover, the exclusion's removal also recognized that while bereavement and major depression were not the same that bereavement could lead to major depression.

In order to provide further clarification, DSM-5 described the differences between grief (bereavement) and major depression. This was especially challenging, as grief and major depression share many characteristics that may appear the same on the surface but are very different. DSM-5 systematically explains grief and major depression in terms of the major feelings a person has, their sense of sadness, feelings of pain, their thoughts, their sense of self-esteem, and suicidal thoughts. The differences are in the specific details.

> *From all the condolences I received when my mother died the oddest one I received was from Sylvia. She said to me, "My mother died 15 years ago and I never got over it. You will never get over it either." At the time I thought that it was an awful thing to say. When a year had gone by and I had not gotten "over it" I thought of what Sylvia said. It is decades later and I still get sad when I think of Mom but I also hear her laughter and still feel her love. Sylvia's words turned out to be the most helpful.*

The grieving person feels a sense of emptiness with pangs or waves of grief associated with thoughts or reminders of the person they have lost. While they may feel pained by these thoughts, they will also be accompanied with positive feelings. It is typical for the person to be preoccupied with memories of the deceased. While the grieving person may feel that they failed the deceased in some way, people who are grieving generally still feel good about themselves. In instances where they experience suicidal thoughts, they are primarily focused on joining the deceased.

The person who is a having a major depressive episode is persistently depressed. They are unhappy and miserable most of the time. They often feel worthless or express self-loathing. When they experience thoughts of suicide, they stem from a negative self-image or being unable to cope with depression.

In grief and major depression, there are deep, painful feelings. However, a person who is grieving also has happy and positive memories. Conversely, the person with major depression experiences no positive feelings.

While these delineations were helpful, they did not take into account the cultural and religious norms for grieving. To address these concerns, a committee of experts at the American Psychiatric Association proposed in 2020 that "Prolonged Grief Disorder" should be added as a new diagnosis based on the assumption that 12 months is an acceptable grieving timeframe, and that to go beyond that amount of time may be problematic. Key to this reconceptualization are that (1) the disturbance causes clinically significant distress or impairment in social, occupational, or other important areas of functioning and (2) the duration of the bereavement reaction clearly exceeds expected social, cultural, or religious norms for the individual's culture and context.[10]

The cultural context for grieving is essential to take into account. Each community has its own ways to grieve a loss. This was most evident when COVID-19 deaths first spiked and funerals were not allowed. We witnessed the great suffering people experienced when they could not engage in the practices that would help ease them through such a difficult time. For some, the depression they experienced was inevitable.

Understanding the depth of a person's depression and the importance of moving forward also means that we cannot allow ourselves to be misled by stereotypes in the media that portray depression as something found only among affluent, non-Hispanic whites. In fact, data shows that Hispanics,

African-Americans, and Asian Americans are more likely to experience depression than non-Hispanic whites. Depression is found in all communities and is so common that each year, one in 15 people has a major depressive disorder. It is also the second leading cause of years lived with disability worldwide, increasing more than 50 percent since 1990.[11] Depression is pervasive.

THE MANY SHADES OF DEPRESSION

Depression is a condition that impacts your mood, frame of mind, and temperament to such a degree that it interferes with your daily life. It encompasses several types of conditions (see descriptions following) and, depending on its severity, will impact your ability to handle your daily activities and enjoy your life. The ways in which depression plays out varies from one person to another based on their age, biology, gender, cultural expectations and values, life experiences, and events in that person's life that may have triggered the episode.

Depression can be found in all communities, and it may occur at any point in a person's life. The consequences of teenage depression are something that should concern us all. Every year, more Latinas under 18 attempt suicide than any other group of girls. This should be unacceptable, yet those numbers have remained the same for decades.

At the other end of the spectrum, some of our older men and women have all the symptoms of depression, but their symptoms are ignored. Instead, their suffering is attributed to growing older or being confused. If we spent more time with them, we might be surprised to find out that they are alone, no one is taking care of them, and that they are, in fact, clinically depressed. We have much to learn about depression across age ranges.

According to the World Health Organization, there are 300 million people worldwide with depression. Throughout the Americas, there are 48 million people with depression and nearly 18 million of those are in the United States.[12] The percent of people with moderate or severe depressive symptoms in the past two weeks varies by age, with the highest rate of 12.3 percent for ages 40 to 59. Across all age groups, women have significantly higher rates than men.[13] In 2014, an estimated 6.7 percent (15.7 million) of adults in the United States had at least one major depressive episode in the past year.[14]

Depression is a common condition. As revealed by these statistics, many more people described depressive symptoms than what was expected. The good news is that there are ways you can manage your life to reduce the likelihood that you will become depressed and, if you are diagnosed with depression, increase your likelihood of getting better with treatment.

TYPES OF DEPRESSION

There are several types of depression found in adults: these include major depression, persistent depressive disorder, perinatal depression, seasonal affective disorder, premenstrual dysphoric disorder, psychotic depression, and difficult to treat depression.[15]

Major Depression (Major Depressive Disorder or Clinical Depression)

When you have a major depression, your relationships with others, your family life, your work, and the pleasurable parts of your life seem to grind to a halt. You cannot do nor do you want to do the things you normally would enjoy. While there are moments like this in all of our lives, one major difference in major depression is the amount of time that these symptoms last. You may be depressed if for at least two weeks, you lose your ability to work, sleep, study, eat, and enjoy life. This is not a momentary event but one that is ongoing, with feelings of sadness present nearly every day. In this situation, people lack the energy and desire to move forward in their life. For some people, this type of major depression may occur once in their lifetime (single episode), while for others it may occur at different points in their lives (recurrent).

Persistent Depressive Disorder (Also Called Dysthymia)

Anna and Edgar were known among their family and friends as a very hardworking couple. They always seemed to be working. Anna was busy trying to help people learn new skills while Edgar worked long hours at his small business. Their marriage of many years had grown from the friendship that had brought them together. And yet when Anna looked at Edgar she saw a man who seemed different from the one she had married; sometimes he even seemed noticeably anxious. Over the years Anna felt an increasing heaviness in their lives that she did not understand. Those were usually the times when Edgar would get anxious and was not even interested in being sexually intimate. One night when they were having dinner, Edgar looked at her and blurted out, "I am so depressed and have been that way all of my life." Anna was astonished and responded, "How could that be? I never saw you being sad or crying and we have been together for a long time." And as the tears welled up in his eyes he continued to look down at his plate and said, "You are not with me all day. I have been depressed all my life . . . it has been that way all of my life . . . I just learned how to hide it."

In this case, a person has a depressed mood on most days and has felt that way for at least two years. Although it may not be as severe as major depression, dysthymia usually lasts longer. Dysthymia is sometimes difficult to diagnose because the symptoms the person experiences are not as disabling as in a major depressive disorder. At times, the person is able to do some of what he or she has to do, even though their negative feelings linger. Some people with dysthymia may also have episodes of major depression throughout their life.

Perinatal Depression (Formerly Postpartum Depression)

This condition presents itself as much more serious than "baby blues," which refer to relatively mild depressive and anxiety symptoms that typically clear within two weeks after delivery. Perinatal depression can occur during pregnancy or after delivery. Feelings of extreme sadness, anxiety, and exhaustion make it difficult for women experiencing this type of depression to continue to perform their daily tasks. New mothers may be unable to care for themselves and/or for their babies.

In the Hispanic community, where larger families are more common and having children is celebrated, it is particularly difficult to accept that there is a type of depression that some women experience during pregnancy or soon after giving birth. For some, perinatal depression is unimaginable because of the cultural belief that being pregnant and having a baby always brings great happiness. But that is a belief that is not true for the 10 to15 percent of women who find the perinatal period to be otherwise.[16] This is a complicated time for some women because they are undergoing many changes in their lives. These include all of the adjustments that must be made due to their body's recent changes, as well as the new needs that occur when adding another member to the family. At the same time, the hormones in the mother's body are going through major fluctuations.

Seasonal Affective Disorder (SAD)

When Ileana told me about her husband, I could only imagine how hard her life had been. While their family and friends saw them as the perfect couple, Ileana knew that their life was a lot more complicated than it appeared. Every winter, especially around the holidays, José would become moody. As the days progressed, those moods would give way to a depression that would make it impossible for him to enjoy the life they had built together. José would just get lost in the fog that seemed to envelop his mind. Ileana felt helpless as she watched the man she loved drown in his winter depression once again.

SAD is characterized by the onset of depression during the winter months, when there is less natural sunlight. This depression generally lifts during spring and summer. Winter depression returns every year in seasonal affective disorder. During this time, the person will want to withdraw from social interactions and will have increased sleep and weight gain.

People with seasonal affective disorder find that as natural sunlight decreases in the winter, their symptoms of depression increase. This is a disorder in which we know that light plays a critical role.

Premenstrual Dysphoric Disorder (PMDD)

This is a serious condition with disabling symptoms such as irritability, anger, depressed mood, sadness, suicidal thoughts, appetite changes, bloating, breast tenderness, and joint or muscle pain. It is not to be confused with premenstrual syndrome (PMS), which is quite common and usually exhibits mild symptoms.

Psychotic Depression

This form of depression occurs when a person experiences severe depression in addition to some form of psychosis. This means that the person may have disturbing false fixed beliefs (delusions). Additionally, they may experience hearing or seeing upsetting things that others cannot hear or see (hallucinations). Their psychotic symptoms, i.e., delusions or hallucinations, typically have a depressive "theme," such as delusions of guilt, poverty, or illness.

Difficult to Treat Depression (DTD)

This is a new category that was developed as part of an international consensus statement by a group of global psychiatrists and published in the *Journal of Affective Disorders* in 2020.[17] The previous category was treatment resistant depression, but this term was discarded for many reasons, particularly since it blamed the disorder itself or the individual for not improving. DTD is "depression that continues to cause significant burden despite usual treatment efforts."[18]

Obtaining a professional diagnosis is essential in order to receive the treatment that will produce the greatest benefits. The recommended treatment may vary for each person, but psychotherapy, i.e. talk therapy, is generally the best treatment option for mild to moderate depression. For more severe cases, a combination of medication and psychotherapy may provide the optimal results. It is up to the clinician and the person receiving treatment to determine the specific therapy and medication that will work best.

DEPRESSION AND SUICIDE

This time Teresa felt different. She seemed to be sinking deeper into her negative feelings. Orlando, her husband, and all of her children knew that Teresa was not okay. Every attempt they made to help her seemed instead to push her deeper into the abyss of sadness that seemed to be engulfing her. Teresa looked at her house and saw how it was increasingly messy with her papers spread all over the kitchen counters. And although she wanted to, Teresa was unable to get out of her bed in the morning, even when she knew she had to take her children to school before she went to work at the job she had never particularly liked. Orlando did not know what to do and became petrified when Teresa said, "I feel like driving the car into a wall."

New longitudinal research on depression followed people over a long period of time. The data showed that 2 percent of the people treated for depression on an outpatient basis died by suicide, whereas for those who had been treated on an inpatient basis, the rate was higher, at 4 percent. The gender differences in the study were quite striking: 7 percent of the men with a history of depression died by suicide and just 1 percent of the women succumbed to suicide.[19]

While only a small percentage of people with depression commit suicide, more than half of the people who do so have depression. Suicide is a major issue in the United States for both men and women, and it remains the 8th leading cause of death for people of all ages. It is a problem for young people but also an issue among those over 65. Across all categories, more men than women commit suicide, with firearms used in about half of all suicides.

From 1999 to 2006 in the United States there was a steady 1 percent increase in suicide. From 2006 through 2017, the rate increased by 2 percent each year. In 2018, more than 48,000 people died by suicide. Additionally in 2018, 10.7 million adults seriously thought about trying to kill themselves. Of those, 3.3 million made a plan, and 1.4 million tried to kill themselves but were unsuccessful.[20] As a result, the National Institute of Mental Health (NIMH) pledged to reduce the suicide rate by 20 percent by 2025.

According to NIMH, if you are concerned that someone is at risk of harming themselves, here are some specific things you can do to try to prevent a person from committing suicide:

1. When communicating with the person, ask "Have you thought about hurting yourself?" If the person says yes, ask if there is a specific plan already in mind.
2. If possible, try to make the person safer by reducing access or disabling the lethal means that were mentioned.
3. Listen as best you can to really hear what the person is saying.
4. Connect them to the 24-hour National Suicide Prevention Lifeline's 1-800-273-TALK (8255) or the Crisis Text Line's number (741741), or if the person is a veteran, the Veterans Crisis Line is 1-800-273-8255 and press 1. These are good resources to keep on your phone. Encourage the person to contact a trusted individual such as a family member, friend, spiritual advisor, or mental health professional.

5. Stay in touch with the person as best you can to give reassurance and to follow up.

These steps are extremely helpful and may prevent some suicides. They will not prevent all suicides. Suicide continues to be a major public health problem.

DEPRESSION AND ITS RELATIONSHIP TO DIABETES AND HEART DISEASE

Our primary task is to care for all of our health conditions. In most circumstances, getting better requires us to take certain actions. This can be especially challenging when someone is depressed because one of their symptoms may be an inability to get things done. Being depressed definitely makes it more difficult to do the things we want to and should do. Most health care providers are aware that they must treat depression along with any other health conditions that may be present.

The relationship between depression and other ongoing health conditions has been well documented. We know that if you have diabetes, for instance, you are more likely to also have depression. The same is also true for people with heart problems.

Diabetes

If you have type 2 diabetes and depression, the causal relationship between these conditions goes in both directions. Depression may increase the likelihood of having type 2 diabetes, but it is also true that having type 2 diabetes increases the likelihood that you will be diagnosed with depression.[21] Changes in a person's blood sugar levels, whether they are spikes or drops, can change a person's mood, ability to focus, and energy level.

Coronary Heart Disease (CHD)

"Thirty years of epidemiological data indicate that depression does predict the development of heart disease," said Jesse C. Stewart, Ph.D., an associate professor of psychology in the School of Science at Indiana University-Purdue University Indianapolis (IUPUI).[22] If you have coronary heart disease, you are three times more likely to be diagnosed with depression than someone without CHD. Depressive symptoms also increase the likelihood that someone with a broad range of heart problems will have a heart attack or require hospitalization for heart problems. Without a doubt, it is essential to manage the depressive symptoms of people with conditions that can involve sudden reduced blood flow to the heart.

Regardless of the type of heart problem someone experiences (coronary heart disease, unstable angina, heart attack, heart failure, or recuperation from coronary bypass surgery), researchers have found that 15 to 20 percent of those with a heart problem have a major depressive disorder. Additionally, an even greater percentage of that group shows signs of milder depression. In another study, researchers concluded that "depression could be a risk factor for heart disease or stroke and suggested that physicians pay close attention to depressive symptoms in older adults."[23] Depression is important to take into account for the full recovery of a person after a cardiac event.

Broken heart syndrome, also called stress-induced cardiomyopathy or takotsubo cardiomyopathy, is a heart condition that exemplifies the connections between depression and heart disease.[24] In the past, it was common to misdiagnose broken heart syndrome as a heart attack because they shared similar symptoms and some test results. However, one major difference between these two conditions was that in broken heart syndrome, there was no evidence of blockage of the heart arteries. Furthermore, blood tests did not show signs of heart damage, and even the EKG was different than it was for someone who was having a heart attack. The good news is that most people recover from broken heart syndrome.

Consideration has been given to the theory that some of the hormones related to stress, which can be a precursor to depression, may have an impact on the heart as well. For a while, it was unclear whether depression actually caused heart problems. However, most still agreed that the two are definitely related and that health care providers must focus on treating both conditions. More recent research has made it clear that there are "shared mechanisms between coronary heart disease and depression."[25]

Significant progress has been made in uncovering the biological mechanisms that explain the connection between depression and CHD. The very chemicals that our body releases when we are stressed have been identified as the link between the two conditions.[26] Some hormones related to stress also have an impact on the heart. While we do not have all the facts, you can be certain that chronic psychological stress is not good for your heart.

In addition to diabetes and heart disease, depression is linked to a range of other conditions. Bits of information are constantly emerging to help us better understand these connections and care for ourselves. One thing is certain: having the additional diagnosis of depression increases the likelihood that you will have an unfavorable outcome. No matter what type of depression and what other health conditions a person may have, it is crucial that they take action to get better as soon as possible.

People with symptoms of depression may find it tough to seek help. A person may feel that only by dragging himself or herself into action can anything be done, and that is okay. Sometimes that is the only way to start.

HOW DEPRESSION IMPACTS YOUR BODY, MIND, AND SPIRIT

Part of the problem with our understanding of depression is that we use the word to cover a broad range of experiences. Sometimes, when we are down, we use the word "depressed" to describe how we feel and confuse that with actual depression. Depression is much more than the sadness you feel because you did not get the offer you expected or the gift you wanted.

Being sad and staying sad for weeks at a time can be a sign of a more serious situation. Feeling unhappy is different from major depression, which you may experience either once in your life or as a recurring event that exhausts your emotional resources, creating a vacuum that consumes all hope and breeds despair. This more wide-ranging form of depression drains those who experience it, as well as the people closest to them, of the energy to take the actions they must perform to get better.

Over time, depression distorts more and more aspects of a person's life as the negative feelings and inability to get things done becomes increasingly embedded in their life. Someone who is severely depressed will experience a profound sadness that overwhelms and immobilizes their life.

Since health is about the wellness of the body, mind, and spirit, it is crucial to use that framework to understand what we are experiencing so that we can take the necessary steps to get better. The signs and symptoms of depression[27] available from the National Institute of Mental Health are explained below in clusters that are consistent with a more comprehensive view of depression.

Body (unintended changes)

Sleep: You are no longer able to sleep the way you used to. The amount of sleep you get each night and/or the quality of that sleep has changed. You may sleep more hours or you may find that you can only sleep for a few hours at a time. It may be difficult for you to go to sleep or to stay asleep. Change is the key factor. You find that unlike your usual pattern, you are waking up early in the morning or oversleeping.

Food: The amount of food you eat has changed, even though you did not intend for that to happen. You may eat significantly more than usual, or you may eat a lot less. Be mindful if you experience an unintended change in weight: some people with depression gain weight and others lose weight.

Decreased energy or fatigue: You no longer have the energy to do anything, even activities you once enjoyed.

Move or talk more slowly: You notice that you are moving or talking more slowly than usual.

Pain: Your body may not feel good. You may have ongoing aches and pains, headaches, cramps, or digestive problems that do not disappear and do not seem to have a physical cause.

Mind (not working well; not at peace)

Persistent sadness, anxiety, or "emptiness": You are not just sad for the moment; the sadness lasts for extended periods of time. At other times, you may feel anxious or empty. Your mind is not at rest. At different times, you may feel sad, anxious, or even as if you have no feelings at all.

Grouchiness or irritability: You have a short temper and find that you get annoyed easily.

Feeling restless or having trouble sitting still: Sometimes you have difficulty being in one place and have a need to move around.

Loss of interest or pleasure in hobbies and activities: It has become difficult for you to find anything to do that will give you pleasure. Even the things that you liked to do no longer seem enjoyable, including sexual intimacy.

Your mind is unclear: You have difficulty concentrating, remembering, or making decisions. You are not able to think the way you once did. You cannot focus on anything, the details are lost, your thoughts get muddled, and, when given choices, you have trouble deciding what you want to do. Trying to make a decision is difficult.

Spirit: (diminished, not in a good place)

Hopelessness or pessimism: You feel that hope has vanished from your life and that life will not get better.

Guilt, worthlessness, helplessness, or feeling unworthy: You feel that things have gone awry in your life, and it is your fault. You feel that you are not worthy of anything good in life, or that there is nothing you can do to improve your life situation.

Death: You have thought about ending your life or have actually tried to end your life.

Go over this list carefully. Consider whether you have experienced unintended changes in how your body functions, feel that your mind is not working as well as it has in the past, and that your spirit feels diminished and burdened with despair. If you have experienced some or all of these symptoms for more than two weeks, there are steps you can to take to get better. First, speak with your health care provider to rule out any physical health problems. If there are no physical issues, you will benefit from seeing a mental health professional who can help you sort through your feelings, emotions, family life, and work life.

Keep in mind that our thoughts, feelings, and behaviors are incredibly complex. In order to understand what makes them unique for each of us, we have to examine all of the pieces that make us do what we do and feel what we feel. To fully understand depression, you must know more about the biology of depression.

YOUR BODY: BIOLOGICAL FACTORS IN DEPRESSION

We all have genes that predispose us or protect us from illness, cells that make up our brain structure, and biochemistry throughout our brain and body. These genes interact with each other and with the external environment that surrounds us.

If you have depression, you have a condition that is interwoven with your genes, your cells, your system for information processing in the brain, your cognition, your temperament, and the events occurring around you. Your depression may be caused by one of these factors or some combination of them. We are just beginning to understand the ways in which these factors affect the body and the changes they generate.

GENES

Your body has about 37 trillion cells. In the center of each cell, there are threadlike structures (chromosomes) that carry your genes. Your genes contain the DNA (deoxyribonucleic acid) that you inherited from your parents.

Genes are the pieces of DNA that have the instructions for creating every part of your body and ensuring that they function properly. The NIH Human Genome Project estimated that humans have between 20,000 and 25,000 genes. All of these pieces working together are responsible for creating the person you are. Yet despite our current understanding of genes, there is still much more to learn.

The process of mapping the human genome was expected to open a new understanding for many conditions, including depression. For this reason, beginning in 2003, there was a massive push to try to sort out a depression gene with the hope that doing so would help identify who would be at risk for depression. As this research continued, it became evident that only a few very rare diseases were caused by a specific gene.

At this point, we know that there is no single gene that causes depression.[28] However, while a particular gene for depression has not been discovered, researchers found that people who had a short version of a particular gene (5-HTTLPR), as opposed to the longer version, were more likely to develop depression when faced with stress.[29] In a genome-wide association study that included 161,640 people with depressive symptoms, researchers identified two variations associated with depressive symptoms.

The same variations were also found in another group of people with depression.[30]

Researchers have now identified hundreds of places in the genome that are irrefutably linked to mental illnesses such as schizophrenia, autism, and depression.[31] By analyzing genes, they identified and refined the connection to major depression. More research is under way to identify other genes that may also have an impact on depression. Yet currently, the specific contribution of genes and the environment to major depressive disorders is still unclear.[32]

Genetic information may help determine which available treatments will work for a particular person. In some cases, certain genes may increase or decrease the likelihood that a medication will be effective. Genes have an effect on how drugs act, whether our body absorbs a drug slowly or quickly, and even how information is processed in the brain. This area of research is called pharmacogenetics. Some of the benefits and side effects of medications that treat depression are probably due to variability in the genes from one person to another.

In addition to understanding what is happening inside a human cell, there is growing interest in environmental factors that affect genes. In these types of studies, researchers focus on external factors that turn genes on or off or change how they function. For example, there is strong evidence that smoking has an impact on genes and how we metabolize drugs. Additionally, research in behavioral epigenetics, the study of how life experiences impact genes, suggests that early life experiences can have a major impact on certain selected genes.

And while some scientists may claim that your genes can tell the entire story of who you are, others believe otherwise. Take the example of identical twins: at first you may have difficulty telling them apart, but the longer you are with them, the more you can see the differences between them in terms of their emotional responses and facial expressions. We've learned from twin studies that even identical genetic code does not produce identical behaviors. This is because experience and environment are factors in shaping our behavior.

Genes play a critical role in determining how well a person can adapt to his or her environment; however, the ways in which that adaptation happens are still unclear. While our genes interact with the experiences we have, we still need to understand how those interactions result in behavioral changes. Stress can actually change our DNA by leaving methyl marks on our DNA and, as a result, can impact the rest of our life. It suffices to say that we have a long way to go before we fully grasp the connection between our genes and depression. It is hoped that the next decade of research will provide the valuable information we need to understand the interactions between genetic factors, environmental changes, and depression.

It is crucial to remember that "depression does not have a clear pattern of inheritance in families. While people who have a parent or sibling with depression are more likely to develop depression many people who develop depression do not have a family history of the disorder and many people with an affected relative never develop the disorder."[33]

BRAIN

The central nervous system is comprised of the brain and the spinal cord. The brain is connected to the spinal cord, which is filled with nerves that provide a two-way pathway allowing your body and brain to communicate with each other. As a result, the brain is one of the major control centers responsible for the ways in which you interact with everything around you.

The brain includes the brainstem, cerebellum, cerebrum and the limbic system. The brain stem controls body functions that you do not have to think about, such as breathing and heart rate. It also links the brain to the spinal cord. The cerebellum gives you balance and the ability to coordinate your movements. It is the part of the brain that coordinates your movement by piecing together information from your eyes, ears, and muscles.

The cerebrum is the largest part of the brain. It is made up of two halves, also known as hemispheres. These hemispheres are connected to each other by a thick bundle of nerves called the *corpus callosum*. Each hemisphere has four sections, or lobes, and each one controls a specific function. The sections in the front are the frontal lobes and are responsible for a person's executive functions. This includes your ability to think, plan, reason, organize, have abstract thoughts, and exercise self-control.

Deep inside the brain is the limbic system. This is a complex set of nerves, networks, and structures that influence emotions (fear, pleasure, anger), motivation (hunger, sex, nurturing), and memories. The limbic system includes the hypothalamus,

thalamus, hippocampus, and amygdala. Each one of these has a specific role.

The hypothalamus is the size of an almond and controls eating, sleeping, and your body temperature. The thalamus relays information to the other parts of the brain, while the hippocampus is responsible for memory and more complex cognitive functions. The amygdala is the part of the brain that detects threats and prepares for emergencies. It plays a crucial role in processing social signals, such as facial expressions, particularly fearful ones.

Researchers are increasingly investigating the role of the amygdala in depression. Your "gut reaction" is believed to be the product of the amygdala. The amygdala is your personal gatekeeper, responsible for processing and recalling emotional reactions and is key to your social behavior. Earlier research indicates that, regardless of gender or age, people with a larger amygdala reported having more substantial and complex social networks.[34] Recent research has confirmed that the size of this social network can be predicted by the brain structure and functions of the amygdala.[35]

We are also learning more about how stress affects the brain. Stress disrupts the normal interaction between the hypothalamus, the pituitary gland, and the adrenal glands. When communication between these glands is no longer synchronized, a person is more likely to have depressive symptoms.

The brain also has many kinds of cells, but the most important ones are the nerve cells, or neurons. Your thoughts and emotions result from signals that pass from one neuron to the next. Sometimes a problem can arise in the area between neurons, called the synapse, that can make it challenging to transmit information from one neuron to another. These problems may be due to chemicals known as neurotransmitters, which are chemical messengers that play a vital role in the communications between nerve cells in the brain. Some examples of these neurotransmitters include serotonin, norepinephrine, dopamine, histamine, GABA (gamma-aminobutyric acid), acetylcholine, and glutamate.

The role of each of these chemicals is unique. For example, GABA neurons are related to the acquisition, storage and extinction of fear. In an extensive review of GABA, it was found that a GABA deficiency is a hallmark of major depression.[36] The role of serotonin, however, is incredibly complex. It appears that people who have depression do not have the proper amount of this neurotransmitter: some have too much, and others have too little. Currently, there is no test that can easily determine how much serotonin needs to be available for good mental health.

Technically, depression is not a disease of the brain but, rather, a disorder involving how the brain functions and processes information. That is why when people say that depression is "all in someone's head," they are only partially wrong. If there are problems in parts of the brain, it may affect some of the behaviors associated with neurological and psychiatric disorders. Since we process information in the brain, when those processes are not working well, we may develop all sorts of conditions.

Research on the brain and how it functions has been advanced by our ability to use brain scans to measure the structure of the brain, blood flow, and levels of oxygen and glucose. While brain scans are not yet used as a tool for diagnosis, the additional information they provide has helped us revise and expand our knowledge of the brain.

Brain activity, as measured by existing technology, does not give us clear-cut answers. Brain scans of love-struck, drug-addicted, and obsessive-compulsive people all look the same. While the feelings one experiences and their corresponding brain scans can change based on the situation, these images may also be very similar to the brain scans of people in very different settings.[37]

Numerous challenges still remain in the study of the brain and how it affects depression. Cultural neuroscience is a growing field of investigation that attempts to explain the ways culture influences brain development. This does not imply that a brain from one culture is better than a brain from another; instead, it demonstrates that there are differences from culture to culture regarding how people process information.

We are still learning how to measure the brain, how to interpret the images of the brain, and what factors can change how the brain works. All of this new information needs to be carefully analyzed in order to determine the impact that changes in brain function have on depression. Research in this field will be invaluable toward the development of new treatment options.

HORMONES

Hormones are the chemical messengers produced by your body. They are part of your endocrine system and control and regulate the activity of certain cells and organs. Hormones work slowly and impact growth and development, how your body gains energy from what you eat, sexual function, reproduction, and mood.[38] When it comes to your feelings and your ability to think, hormones play significant roles.

Various studies have been conducted to demonstrate how hormones alter women's moods. During adolescence, pregnancy, and menopause, women experience hormonal changes that can lead to depressive states. During these times, shifts are present in both estrogen and testosterone levels. Research has shown that during the first two years after menopause, women have a greater risk of having a major depressive episode. However, it is unclear whether this is due to hormonal changes or life events.

While researchers have been investigating women in their late forties to early fifties due to their hormonal changes, few studies have analyzed the hormonal changes that men experience during this same time of life. The lack of data on men reflects the bias that only women are impacted by hormonal changes. We know very little about how hormones impact men as they get older. We do know that men with decreased levels of testosterone had increased levels of depression and anxiety. This often occurs in the same age range when men are more likely to commit suicide.

Although the study of the effect of hormones on our behavior is very complicated[39] there are at least two hormones that need to be considered because of their relationship to depression— cortisol and oxytocin.

Cortisol plays a pivotal role in depression because it is the hormone associated with the ways we handle stress. Like stress itself, cortisol has a good side and a not-so-good side. Cortisol can prepare you for challenges, but too much of it can cause all sorts of complications. When you are in a stressful situation, cortisol is one of the chemicals your body releases to prepare your immune system to respond to stress. After the situation has passed, cortisol communicates to your immune system that it can relax. However, when you have too much stress in your life, cortisol remains in your system and the cells in your immune system stop responding. Over time, your cortisol level does not return to normal, explaining why you may begin to experience problems due to constant, high stress.

Much has also been written about oxytocin. This is a hormone that behaves like a neurotransmitter in the brain and has drawn interest among health researchers and the general public. This hormone, sometimes referred to as the "cuddle hormone," has received popular attention because it seems to have an impact on how people relate to one another. Specifically, oxytocin is involved in the behaviors that connect people to each other. In a recent study focusing on the relationship between oxytocin and depression, researchers found that oxytocin impacts a person's response to stress. As a result, this hormone could also have an effect on depression.[40]

MICROBIOME

The human microbiome consists of the 100 trillion microbes (composed of bacteria, bacteriophage, fungi, protozoa and viruses) that live mainly in the gut. These microbes are essential for health and wellness and play a critical role in digestion and your immune system, as well as many other body functions.

For more than a decade, researchers have worked to uncover the connection between the gut and the brain. The gut and the brain are connected by a two-way highway that communicates through microbes to maintain a person's health. Current research is examining gut bacteria to develop new medicines for the brain.[41] The complete relationship between the microbiome and a person's health is still being deciphered.

In summary, your body contains many components that could trigger depression, but we still are not sure what the causes are.[42] It is unlikely that your depression is related solely to your genes. Depression may also result from a malfunctioning of the brain or reflect a chemical imbalance in your neurotransmitters, your hormones, or your microbiome.

What we do not know is whether depression is caused by one biological factor or a combination of these biological factors, or whether the depression causes these malfunctions. By eventually finding the answers to these fundamental questions, we can significantly improve our understanding of depression and develop better treatments.

We do know that depression is more than a chemical imbalance; it is a condition that alters your mind and spirit.

YOUR MIND AND SPIRIT: CONNECTIONS TO DEPRESSION

Our knowledge about the connection between depression and the mind and spirit is challenged. The objectivity which is essential to research can miss the richness of the persons subjective experience. To understand the mind and spirit we rely on what a person says and does to attempt to grasp their feelings and emotions.

> David explained, "You know how you feel when you come down from doing Molly?[43] Well imagine waking up in the morning and feeling like that every day of your life. That is what it feels like every morning when I wake up."

I asked Edith how she had adjusted to being home with her husband for several months because of the COVID-19 stay-at-home precautions. She paused and said, "The day goes well when I can get through it... when I see the faces of people who have helped . . . the personal courage of so many has been absolutely remarkable. I think of my own life and I get depressed."

Our feeling and emotions frame our lives. Ironically, when we ask how a person is doing, we rarely attempt to know how they are truly feeling or what is going on in their life. "How are you?" in all of its iterations is the standard greeting we give each other. The response is the programmed, "Fine. And you?" All is good when a person responds with "Good," "Great," or "OK." To hear a less than positive but honest response creates an uncomfortable pause. The ritual has been broken; the intent was never to know what someone was really feeling or to recognize the emotions that were stirred.

Somehow, we have moved to a place where the norm is to avoid getting involved with the emotions of others. We have opted out of speaking about our emotions. It is not surprising that, as a consequence, we have also learned to create a pseudo self. Facebook, Instagram, and their successors have become platforms for projecting a superficial image rather than who we are and what we truly feel. We edit and curate what we put forward instead of getting closer to our emotions and the emotions of others. We use technology to conceal our feelings for the greater goal of public appeal, and in the process, we lose a defining part of our identities.

Our emotions teach us our first lessons about life. Evidence shows that babies as young as four months old learn to read the emotions of those around them and communicate basic needs.[44] We quickly learn who to love and who to fear. We learn from those around us and those who leave us alone. Our emotions exist to help us thrive and are powerful components in our life toolbox.

Many strive to shut down their feelings and emotions as if doing so is a badge of success, when in fact quite the opposite is true. Acknowledging our feelings and emotions, as well as the role they play in our lives, is at the heart of success and being happy. We recognize this when we embrace the need for emotional intelligence (EQ).[45]

Emotional intelligence refers to our ability to understand our own emotions and those of others. Recent research proposes a nine-layer model of emotional intelligence. At the base are the emotional stimuli that we encounter every day, and at the pinnacle is emotional unity.[46] EQ enables us to manage ourselves, our lives, and our relationships. Many of these skills are learned and unlearned throughout life.

No matter what level of emotional intelligence we have, we all need to recognize our own feelings and emotions and realize the major role they have in understanding and managing depression.

FEELINGS

Alicia was someone who had gone through life ignoring her feelings. When asked how she was doing she would answer, "Fine." She plowed ahead doing what she had to do to get through her very long days. She juggled responsibilities for her children, work, and more

43

family. Her "to-do" lists seemed to grow as fast as she could cross off items. Then one day while watching a movie she found herself crying uncontrollably. At that moment she realized that all could not be fine.

Everyone has feelings; they are part of our individual consciousness. Feelings are specific to each person. It does not matter if no one else seems to understand your feelings–even if you don't either. It only matters that you acknowledge those feelings and understand that they are very real. When Alicia found herself crying, she took an important first step toward accepting that she had feelings that she had not previously considered.

Recognizing that we have feelings is key to grasping what pushes us in different directions. Each of us consciously encounters life through our feelings; they are our self-perceptions. We experience the people, events, and environment around us through our feelings. When you walk down a dark alley, you may feel safe, hot, cold, or a sense of foreboding. Feelings include that intuitive "gut sense" that something is not right that may prompt you to change directions and avoid that alley.

Depression and other issues can result when people go to the extremes of how they handle their feelings, which can range from either totally giving into their feelings (all-in) or pretending they do not exist (ignore). In all-in, feelings take over the person and overpowers them. For example, a person who starts to feel anxious holds on to their anxiety to the point that it becomes all-encompassing, effectively immobilizing them. In all-in, a person completely gives into their feelings to the exclusion of anything else.

The ignore approach occurs when a person pushes their feelings aside by either pretending that they have no feelings, numbing themselves to their feelings or trying to diminish the importance of what they feel. This approach provides an immediate way to handle a difficult situation and serves as a coping mechanism. Nevertheless, at best it is a short-term, temporary fix. The ignore approach makes a person miss out on the valuable information that feelings can provide. If ignore becomes a habit, complications are likely to occur as feelings are real and can bubble up to the surface of our lives in ways that are unexpected and often counterproductive. Depression is one of those ways.

> *Juan was always busy looking for the next big deal and trying to get new clients. He was enthusiastic and very successful. When he told me about his depression I asked him how it was that no one knew about it. He laughed and said because he ignored his feelings. Since he was known to get grouchy people just thought he was having a bad day. He had learned to ignore what he felt. In fact, he was miserable and often thought about ending his life.*

Juan experienced a constant feeling of sadness, regardless of his achievements—he chose the ignore strategy. The world only saw one aspect of his life and had no idea that Juan led a secret life of anguish. There is a limit to how much you can ignore and sweep under the proverbial rug; at some point, the bulge will grow so large that it blocks your path, giving you no choice but to deal with it.

Feelings are our first source of information about a situation.

But where do all of these feelings come from? They are molded by exposure to experiences early in life and our choice of what we have learned from the experience. The greatest challenge has been to find a positive way to leverage our feelings.

The very subjective nature of our feelings makes them valuable. We have to recognize the experiences that drive our emotions, which are ultimately revealed by our feelings. This is the area where feelings and emotions become intertwined.

EMOTIONS

While feelings and emotions can overlap, when it comes to emotions, what generates them is not as clear. Emotions can come from an experience we remember or one we want to forget. Some neuroscientists consider emotions to be less subjective than feelings because to them, emotions result from the ways your brain and body respond to external or internal stimuli.[47] The objective measures that scientists evaluate are your sweat (EDA/GSR), your brain waves (EEG, fMRI), your heart rate (ECG), and how big or small your pupils get (pupil dilation).

Evidence shows that measurements can be taken that link a person's responses to certain emotions. These measurements are valuable because they help us identify changes that occur as the result of things that trigger an emotional response. Sometimes you are aware of what the trigger is, and sometimes you are not.

Think of your emotional response when you see someone cry. We tend to pair crying with the emotion of sadness, but that does not apply in all cases. For certain people, crying is a sign of deep emotion, but, depending on the person and situation, the emotion that generates this response could have a variety of sources. These tears may be rooted in joy, frustration, or regret; they may even serve the sole purpose of getting a desired reaction from those who are watching.

> *Yvette had put up with Oscar's screaming and yelling and demanding behavior for years, but one day she had had enough and decided it was time to file for divorce. When she told Oscar what she had done, he became very quiet and began to sob. Yvette felt terrible and it made her feel guilty that she had initiated divorce proceedings.*

Oscar's tears were real, but they were not connected to either sadness or the end of their marriage. His tears were tears of frustration because Yvette had gotten the upper hand in the court proceedings since she had filed first. Whatever empathy Oscar's tears had stirred up in Yvette, was obliterated once she learned which emotions had actually generated his tears.

When it comes to depression, the roles of different emotions are difficult to tease out. A notable example is the experience of shame or guilt. Both are negative emotions, and at a superficial level, they seem to be related. However, research shows that shame (feeling bad about ourselves), not guilt (feeling bad about our action), has an impact on depression.[48]

In order to manage our emotions, we must recognize them accurately; yet by their very nature, we are sometimes unaware of what sparked them. Very often, people do not have the words to describe their emotions and end up making statements that downplay or misrepresent what they are experiencing. They may say, "I am tired," when a more accurate statement would be "I don't enjoy anything in my life anymore."

Negative emotions about ourselves can lead to lower self-esteem. In turn, these feelings can lead to hopelessness and pessimism. And when these emotions linger or become our predominant emotion, we are on the path to depression.

In order to prevent this process, we must learn how to handle our emotions in a way that is productive and joyful. Emotions are complex and impact our body, mind, and spirit in formidable ways that may not always be obvious. The 2020 call for a biopsychosocial model[49] by some leading practitioners brings to the forefront how the body and immune system are so interrelated with our emotions and the psychological effects of our social surroundings. Research is being pursued with the goal of developing a long-term strategy to increase our awareness of the sources of our emotions, as well as determining how they are coupled with feelings. Sometimes, our mental wellness will depend on reinforcing that bond; at other times, it will require uncoupling.

I once saw an interview of an actor who was asked how she was able to do a sex scene so intensely and convincingly with an actor she did not like. She answered that what she was showing was the intensity of her dislike. What people thought she was feeling was different from her reality.

It is easy to misinterpret the expression on someone's face because the ways people show their emotions vary significantly from one person to another. Moreover, our ability to read facial expressions is not as good as we think and is often tinted by the lens of our own culture and experiences.

Most people believe that they can tell when someone is sad

or suffering from depression. However, the reality is that we often cannot tell who is in the midst of a depressive episode just by their facial expressions. A person may appear to be the life of the party, but upon returning home, their smiles disappear and the hollowness within them returns. Rather than admitting that there is something wrong, people who are depressed typically conceal their feelings in public, only to return to the despair of their lives when they are alone.

There is no single image that encompasses all of the feelings and emotions that are connected to depression. You cannot simply look at someone and understand the feelings and emotions they are experiencing. In fact, many cope by covering their despair with a smile.

In order to grasp the depths of depression, we need to recognize the roles of our feelings and emotions, which are played out in daily life through our thoughts and behaviors. Our self-esteem is connected to our feelings and emotions and is a significant driver of depression.

SELF-ESTEEM

Self-esteem relates to your perception of yourself and includes your overall sense of self-worth. Having high self-esteem means that you believe you are a person with good characteristics and values. However, even highly successful people can have very low self-esteem. Self-esteem is essential for our mental well-being. People with healthy self-esteem are resilient and have the skills to handle difficult situations.

Healthy self-esteem means that you like and value yourself

regardless of the imperfections that make you human. Healthy self-esteem is very different from someone who has such an inflated sense of self as to be called narcissistic. People who are narcissistic overestimate their attractiveness and intelligence, lack shame, and tend to be very competitive. They are the opposite of a person with high self-esteem, since they fail to openly acknowledge that they are not perfect. In contrast, someone with high self-esteem will recognize that there are areas of their personality that they want to change or improve. People with healthy self-esteem are optimistic, are more likely to be satisfied with their lives, and experience lower rates of depression, worthlessness, and hostility.[50]

Conversely, people with low self-esteem have a low or negative view of themselves. They are likely to devalue their appearance, judgement, intelligence, and most aspects of their lives. People with low self-esteem often lack confidence and feel bad about who they are. As a result, they do not handle criticism well, tending to either withdraw or get hostile when given feedback.

For many years, researchers believed that there was a link between low self-esteem and depression, but they were not certain about the nature of that connection. Now we know that this link exists, and it is stronger than some imagined. A recent, major study of studies (meta-analysis) analyzed 77 studies of depression and concluded that low self-esteem predicted depression.[51] Nevertheless, many questioned whether these findings were only relevant to people in the United States or if it also applied to people in other countries.

The researchers Bleidorn and Arslan[52] worked to answer

this fundamental question of whether self-esteem was a valid concept across cultures. In their study, they used an internet sample of 985,937 people ages 16 to 45 in 48 nations to respond to this question. After analyzing the responses from people who lived in the Americas, they found that the results were, in many ways, surprisingly consistent. Throughout the Americas, men had higher levels of self-esteem than women, regardless of age. The major difference between the United States and the rest of the Americas was related to how people's self-esteem changed as they grew older. Self-esteem increased from ages 16 to 50, except in the United States, where it remained constant regardless of age.

While low self-esteem is certainly not conducive to mental well-being, increasing self-esteem has been found to be beneficial for improving depressive symptoms.[53] While we now understand the importance of self-esteem to our mental well-being, our next challenge is to understand how to strengthen it. Fundamentally, we need to understand what shapes our self-esteem. Where does it come from? We know that culture and society, our work, and our relationships are some of the factors that shape self-esteem.

Culture and Society

Culture is beyond language—it defines our daily routines, the ways we eat, our art and music, our values, and just about every other aspect of our lives. Culture influences the events we celebrate and the things we avoid. It contains both myths and realities, which are transmitted through the lessons we learn and affect our perceptions of ourselves and others. For example, the United States' culture is built on a belief of the power of the individual and consequently places a high value on rugged individualism. In many other countries, values are more focused on community.

Everything from media images to police reports emphasizes the fact that the dominant culture of the United States values some people more than others. Generally, those who are non-Hispanic, white, male, tall, and thin are viewed in a more positive light. The more of those characteristics you have, the more positively you are viewed by society. The fewer of those characteristics you have, the more likely you are to be perceived in a negative way. Some of these negative messages are subtle, but many are not. Regardless, they can result in marginalization and even physical harm. To be devalued or undervalued by the dominant culture of your country has a major effect on a person's self-esteem.

The context in which culture unfolds can be very provocative and has an impact across generations. Many texts have been written about the effects of slavery on generations of African Americans' sense of belonging and self-esteem. The United States' history of slavery, as well as the oppression that continued afterward, still reverberates in the lives of African Americans. When it comes to Hispanics or Latinx, their relationship with the United States' culture is complex and compromised for various reasons, some of which are not as obvious as one would think.

Hispanics can trace their heritage to numerous places. Each person's family history follows its own unique path to being part of the United States. In New Mexico, there are Hispanics who can trace their lineage 500 years back to the first Spanish settlers on the continent, and some even have the land grants to prove it. Other families arrived in a variety of ways—some as legal immigrants, refugees, undocumented workers, and through other work programs. Then there are the families who trace their heritage to the results of war, such as the 1848 Treaty of Hidalgo[54] or the 1898 Spanish America War[55] or purchase (the Louisiana Purchase).[56] As a result, people in the Southwest and West, as well as Puerto Ricans, can claim "We did not cross the border, the border crossed us."

Many people in the United States are unaware of these historic events, because the only history they were taught was that of the thirteen colonies. Most history lessons in the United States are narratives that perpetuate the English animosity towards the Spanish.[57] As a result, generations have developed an attitude of superiority and a belief in an American manifest destiny toward Mexico, Latin America, and people of Spanish-speaking origin.

More recently, acrimony toward Hispanics arose in discussions of immigration and bilingual services. When political leaders maligned Hispanics, most of the people who raised their voices in protests were Hispanic. Some Hispanics, however, remained silent because they, too, were the product of the distorted history that most Americans were taught. When the same leadership forced Hispanic children seeking asylum into cages, public outcry was relatively subdued. It was evident that the United States' dominant culture had spread such a negative attitude toward Hispanics that such horrific behavior would be allowed.

The impact of devastating events like these on the self-esteem of Hispanics has been substantial. The Hispanic community's perception and reality of not being valued creates a different kind of stress and produces lasting effects as people try to adapt to the culture of the U.S. Ironically, the first generation of people born in the United States consistently face more problems: they know that they belong, but the United States, the country of their birth, signals otherwise.

It is even more challenging to develop healthy self-esteem when few positive role models look like you. This sense of being different creates significant stress. Researchers have reported that it consistently correlates with sleeping problems, which is a major factor in causing depression.[58] The stress produced from trying to adjust to an intolerant culture is detrimental to a person's physical health, it is also likely to intensify depressive symptoms. And people who feel that they are not valued, who are given social signals that they are different and do not belong, are likely to see themselves as "Ni de aquí Ni de allá" (not from here not from there). For all these reasons, the high rates of depression among Hispanics is not surprising.

Work

People spend most of their waking hours working, either at home or elsewhere. As a result, work ends up being the platform where we gather evidence that can strengthen or weaken our self-esteem.

The work we do and our feelings about our work are major contributors to our self-esteem. Sometimes, this happens in ways that we do not understand. However, we do know that engaging in work that we enjoy and feel good about, builds a person's self-esteem. Evidence shows that the happiest people perform work that they find rewarding,[59] so perhaps it can simply be concluded that when we do what we enjoy, we are less stressed, leading to lower rates of depression.

Ultimately, work is respected and valued in all of its iterations, including work that is done in the home. We also increasingly value unpaid work, and several studies have shown that people who volunteer are both psychologically happier and physically healthier than those who do not volunteer. While some professions may be viewed as more prestigious than others, the value of different types of work is an evolving metric.

The COVID-19 pandemic highlighted that essential workers are present in a broad range of occupations and professions. People who once considered their work to be simply a job realized that their work played an integral role in the fabric of society. Others learned that they had vastly underestimated society's need for the work they did. Each person's self-worth had to be realigned with what they learned about the work they did.

Relationships

Self-esteem first develops in a family context. We realize that many more families than we would like to admit do not cultivate the kind of environment that fosters healthy self-esteem. Some people even spin fantasies about the relationships they have with family members in order to pretend that everything is fine.

The importance of family (blood relatives or not) and of being connected to others is well documented. Communities throughout the world find solace in their extended families to not only help them survive through difficult times but also celebrate all of the events in their lives. The value of family as a source of support and nurturance is essential to all societies.

Self-esteem develops through love and the feeling of being cherished. Findings from across 40 studies emphasize that parents with high self-esteem display more positive interactions with their children.[60] As a result, it is not surprising that parents with healthy self-esteem are more likely to produce healthy self-esteem in their children.

In some families, the contrast in values between their community-oriented heritage and the individualism dominant in the U.S. presents unique challenges for family relationships.[61,62] However, strong family ties are not always as supportive as we would think. Calzada and Sales[63] studied 175 Mexican-origin mothers and found that stronger *familismo* (a strong sense of identification with and loyalty to the nuclear and extended family) actually increased the risk for later depression.

Your feelings, emotions, and self-esteem create a window that reveals how depression can impact your mind and spirit. There are many challenges to developing a healthy self-esteem but you can take several actions on your own to prevent or even lift the fog of depression.

WHAT YOU CAN DO ON YOUR OWN

As we have seen, depression covers a range of conditions that are triggered by a variety of factors. While there are a number of treatment options available (see the next chapter), you can also take many actions on your own. Some of these are ones you may already be familiar with. These need to be reaffirmed, implemented, and followed on a consistent basis. The basics of life need to be approached in a straightforward way that make you stronger and more resilient. When you face doubt in your life, you can use the following self-statements to guide you in strengthening your body, mind, and spirit: embrace the good, refrain from the toxic, and enjoy the waves.

THE GOOD

"Embrace the good" means that we recognize that there are good and bad aspects to everything and that nothing is perfect. Each encounter can have both a positive and a negative side. In order to embrace this concept, we first need to sort out the elements that promote our well-being. This is tough to do because often when we approach situations we do so without much thinking. We rely on the experiences we have had in the past, as well as the lessons we have collected throughout our lifetime. We follow the patterns of our habits because they are the most familiar to us. Some of these actions are conscious, and others are unconscious. Some habits may not be what are best for us, but since they are a familiar track, they can override our better judgement.

The self-statement "embrace the good" guides us to pause, think, and be grateful. Evidence shows that gratitude is positively associated with health and well-being across a wide variety of situations. Thankfully for Latino Americans, recent research reported that they had a greater disposition toward gratitude, which was associated with higher self-esteem and less loneliness.[64]

"Embrace the good" does not mean that we embrace what is good for an extended period of time. Too much of a good thing can be suffocating, overindulgent, and, ironically, just not good for you. Here are some key areas:

Good Relationships

The first relationship you need to embrace and feel good about is the one you have with yourself. This means that you value yourself for who you are and that you are able to have realistic expectations for yourself. Self-esteem grows from your experiences. When your self-esteem is justified, you enjoy mental wellness and take an important step toward reducing the likelihood that you will become depressed.

Self-esteem is also intertwined with the capacity to face the stress of difficult situations and arrive at a healthier place in your life. This capacity is called *resilience*. The combination of self-esteem and resilience makes it possible to get through difficult times.

Self-esteem makes it possible for you to develop healthy boundaries between yourself and others. Embracing the good means that sometimes you say yes, but you must also be able to say no.

An important corollary is that people with healthy self-esteem are just as likely to say that they have a problem as they are to recognize that a problem is not theirs. Problem ownership, which is your awareness of whether a problem is yours or someone else's, is key to having healthy self-esteem. Setting healthy boundaries is fortified by one's ability to accurately assess where the problem actually lies. It is not about saying, "That is not my problem," but rather affirming that sometimes a situation is not within your scope of responsibility and control.

Feeling good about yourself allows you to build relationships based on common values and not because you are trying to compensate for feelings of inadequacy. Healthy connections are key to avoiding or diminishing the effects of depression. In a healthy relationship, both participants give and receive in a way that makes everyone feel that they are taken care of, valued, and respected.

Your ability to feel good about who you are and your ability to do good are the first steps toward cultivating healthy relationships. One recurring theme in research findings is that good relationships are essential to our physical and mental health. There are many benefits to having an active social network, and while these networks are more common among women, they can also improve the lives of men.

Embracing the good in relationships can also protect you from depression and many other conditions. The importance of healthy relationships was further highlighted in the Healthy Women Study,[65] which found that high marital satisfaction increases the likelihood of good health outcomes. Women who rated their relationships high in regard to satisfaction had lower levels of biological, lifestyle, and psychosocial risk factors. In contrast, a poorly-rated marriage was a better predictor of cardiovascular death in women than in men. Based on this data, it was determined that women experienced more physiological responses to marital conflict or disagreement than men did.

There is increasing evidence that religious involvement has a positive impact on a person's life.[66] While many of us understand that faith is important to us, there is sometimes considerable social pressure to devalue the impact of faith with respect to our mental health. Initially, researchers claimed that people felt better when actively practicing their religion because it encouraged and bolstered social ties. A deeper analysis of information from this study showed that, regardless of which factors you took into account, participation in religious activities had a positive effect on depression in both men and women.[67] Additionally, in further research it seemed that, for reasons that could not be identified, religious involvement helped reduce the stress experienced by more recent immigrants to the United States.[68]

We know that frequent attendance at religious services among health care professionals is associated with a lower subsequent risk of death from drugs, alcohol, and suicide.[69] These findings suggest that a correlation exists between frequent attendance at religious services and reduced risk of subsequent death from despair. In this study of 66,492 female registered nurses and 43,141 male health care professionals in the United States, attendance at religious services at least once per week was associated with a 68 percent lower hazard of death from despair among women and a 33 percent lower hazard among men, compared with those who never attended services. The positive role of faith is evident.

The greatest challenge is to do the obvious—to nurture healthy relationships with ourselves and others. This meant that we had to approach our work life and our home life in a different way.

With the emergence of COVID-19, people were overwhelmed because anxiety coupled with depression, especially at a community level, was pervasive. The choice of either leaving home or staying inside was no longer our decision to make. Instead, we had to rethink our most intimate relationships, as well as those that were strained. And the possibility of another wave of "stay-at-home" mandates meant we had to approach both our work and our home life in new and unexpected ways.

Before the COVID-19 outbreak, people worked very hard to achieve work-life balance, yet few did. Most of us felt as if we lived in a perpetual seesaw: not only did it require extra work to achieve this balance, but it was not much fun to strive to be perfectly balanced. It seemed that the more we tried to achieve a work-life balance the more obstacles were thrown in our way. Some people gave up, while others achieved a work-life balance because they had the means to hire others to do certain parts of their job. Countless others just became depressed. To many, the concept of work-life balance was a throwback to another time when people had very compartmentalized lives.

When we examine all of the frustration generated by striving for the impossible goal of a work-life balance, it becomes clear that this path will lead us away from true happiness and fulfillment. Both technology and jobs have drastically changed, and a new model has to be created to align with people's current and future lifestyles. People are now expected to be available 24/7 while simultaneously maintaining a healthy family life. How can this be achieved? The answer lies in each person's evaluation of (1) the demands of their work, (2) their ability to mentally switch channels, and (3) their need for quiet time. We need to create for ourselves a model that is not about balance, but instead, the healthy integration of work and family life.

Good Food

Embracing the good means that you recognize that the food you eat is for nourishment and energy. However, it is just as important to enjoy its various flavors and textures. Eating mindlessly is simply a waste of calories and money; instead, the food that goes into your mouth should be both enjoyable to eat and good for your body. Similarly, the things we drink should be good for us, too. Our bodies are mostly made of water, and we need to stay well-hydrated in order to optimize our bodily functions.

How do you know what is good food? You probably already know the answer to that: most of us know what is good for us and what is not. Fresh fruits, vegetables, beans, unprocessed foods, whole grains, rice, pasta, and even red meat (no hormones or antibiotics added), milk, butter, and cheese are to be embraced in the amounts that are reasonable for you at this point in your life. As you get older, you actually need to eat fewer calories not just because your metabolism slows down, but also because people become less active over time. You want to eat what you need; when you eat more than your body needs, you gain weight.

Just in case you do not know if a certain food is good for you, there are many convenient ways to get this information. The labels on packaged foods and, increasingly, items on restaurant menus provide the nutritional information of your meal. I cannot begin to tell you the number of times that I thought a small container of juice was one serving until I read the label and discovered that it was two or more servings. Even worse, at one point I thought I was drinking juice when it turned out to be flavored water that was loaded with sugar. It took me a moment to realize that an 8-ounce glass, which is quite small, contained 35 grams of sugar. That meant I was having nearly 9 teaspoons of sugar in one small glass (4 grams of sugar = 1 teaspoon sugar). I know we need some sugar for our bodies but that was too much. To save money and calories, embrace drinking plain water. Water is so much better for you.

Good Drugs

You also need to take the medicines that your health care provider prescribes for you. It is just as important to be clear about *how* to take the medications prescribed for you. Too often when people fill their prescriptions they just look at how often they should take their medicine and how much each time. Also be aware of the specific instructions on how to take your medicine, for example, with water or with or without food. Whatever the instructions are, make sure that you understand and follow them. If you do not understand how and when you are supposed to take your medication, ask a pharmacist. It is better to ask questions than for the medication not to work because you are taking it incorrectly.

If you are taking more than one medication, use whatever system works for you (such as a notebook, app, or calendar) to keep track of when you take each of your medications. This will be useful information for you to know and to have for your next visit to your health care provider.

Good Movements

Embracing the good sometimes means doing what you may not like. My mother worked in a factory, but every day she would get up and exercise for 20 minutes before her hard day of work started. On the weekends, she would try to get me to join her. I must admit that even as a five-year-old, I did not like to exercise. I still do not like to exercise, but I do it anyway because I know it is good for me.

The many benefits of movement make it critical that we engage in physical activity for our muscles and joints. Regular exercise is also extremely beneficial for our mental wellness. When it comes to depression, there is very strong evidence that exercise is a means of preventing illness and that it has therapeutic benefits.

While exercise is good for everyone, it is particularly beneficial for people who are depressed. The explanations for these good outcomes range from the impact of exercise on serotonin levels to improved sleep. Exercise is not only good for our muscles and bones but also benefits every other part of our body, including our brain.

While you may look to others for inspiration, you should also be realistic about what you will actually do. Does this mean that you have to run a marathon or compete in an Ironman triathlon? If you can do so in a healthy way, that is fine. But the majority of us need to find some physical activity that we can work into our daily lives. At this point, you may feel that you do not have enough time to dedicate to hours of exercise, and that is perfectly fine. The meaning of "embracing the good" is that you make time for activities that are good for you, and movement is definitely one of them.

The type of activity you do will also vary by your age. At various stages in your life, you will most likely make different choices. Perhaps when you were in your teens, you liked to play team sports. Later in your life, when it got harder to get a group together, you may have preferred to ride a bicycle or go for a walk. Some of us may be lifelong dancers and know that you don't always need a partner. Regardless, the purpose of movement is to stay as active as possible. That does not mean that you have to perform the same activity each time.

Too often, we find women stretching and men lifting weights when in reality, we all need to do some of both. For everybody, the best physical activity will have variety and will engage every part of your body. This means we all need to build our endurance through cardio, enhance our flexibility by stretching, and gain strength by lifting weights.

And when we engage in the activity of our choosing, we do it at the level at which we find ourselves right now. People tend to attempt to restart an activity that they enjoyed in their younger years, trying to pick-up where they had left off years before. However, they often overdo it and injure themselves. You should not expect to immediately be at the same level as when you left off. And, of course, before you add new movements and activity to your routine, be sure to talk to your health care provider to determine whether there are special considerations you need to take into account.

Activity is so good for all of us. While a wide variety of theories exist as to why activity works so well to manage depression, the takeaway is that we all need to figure out how to make it a part of our lives.

Sleep is good

"Embrace sleeping" recognizes the importance of sleeping for mental and physical wellness. In 2020, at least 10 new books were published that focused on sleep. Each book took a different approach, but they all shared a common theme regarding the importance of sleep for good health. Sleep should not be a task that we do when everything else is done on our to-do list. Instead, sleep needs to be a part of planning our day.

Some of us mistakenly believe that when we sleep, our bodies are not doing anything worthwhile. The truth is quite the contrary. When you sleep, your body continues to perform important functions even though you are in a different state of awareness. While you sleep, your body produces key hormones that are essential for your physical and mental health. When you do not get enough sleep or your sleep is low quality, you will experience many negative consequences. For example, women are more likely to have low sexual desire or other sexual problems if they do not get adequate sleep. When we don't sleep enough, we gain weight, get depressed, and cannot think so clearly. Sleep is restorative to our body, mind, and spirit.

Sleep sufficiency and adequacy are critical topics in scientific discussion because of the essential biological functions that occur when a person sleeps, as well as the negative consequences when someone does not get enough sleep. There are now sleep coaches to help people sleep, and some hotels even offer a variety of pillows to enhance guests' sleeping experiences.

The amount of sleep you actually need varies by age (see the chart below).[70] There is increasing evidence that, for most people, sleeping only four to five hours a night causes negative consequences in their body functions and their brain chemistry.

Age	Appropriate Sleep
Newborns (0-3 months):	14-17 hours
Infants (4-11 months):	12-15 hours
Toddlers (1-2 years):	11-14 hours
Preschoolers (3-5):	10-13 hours
School age children (6-13):	9-11 hours
Teenagers (14-17):	8-10 hours
Younger adults (18-25):	7-9 hours
Adults (26-64):	7-9 hours
Older adults (65+):	7-8 hours

Remember that when you do not sleep well, your entire body is thrown into a state of confusion because a healthy body functions on a regular 24-hour cycle of physical, mental, and behavioral changes that respond primarily to light and darkness. This regular cycle is called your *circadian rhythm*, and it is driven by the biological clocks throughout your body. These biological clocks are actually groups of interacting molecules in cells throughout your body. Your brain coordinates all of your body's internal clocks so that they are in sync. When they are out of sync, you are more likely to have symptoms of depression.

Disturbed sleep is found in people who experience depression. It is not clear which comes first—the sleep disturbance or the depression. We also know that lack of sleep is a major risk factor for depression, especially for people who work night shifts because regularly staying up late disrupts their circadian rhythms.

Recent findings suggest that the amount of light you are exposed to between dusk and when you go to sleep is very important. It seems that artificial light from screens (television, computer, video games, cell phone, etc.), especially in the hour before you go to sleep, disrupts the production of hormones associated with sleep and upsets your circadian rhythms.

Based on the recommendations of the National Sleep Foundation, there are several specific actions you can to take to increase the likelihood that you will get a good night's sleep:

- *Keep a schedule:* Create a sleep schedule of when you need to go to sleep and when you need to wake up, even on weekends.
- *Create a routine:* Get your body ready for bed by creating and keeping a sleep time ritual or pattern.
- *Claim a sleep space:* Work to make sure that the location in which you sleep meets your needs in terms of temperature, sound, and light. Your sleeping area should be a sanctuary for you. Sometimes this is as simple as covering your head with your sheet and pretending you hear a soothing sound.
- *Avoid certain substances:* Beware of sleep stealers, such as alcohol and caffeine. At night, when it is close to the time you want to go to sleep, avoid food and drinks with caffeine (this includes chocolate), large meals, and drinks with alcohol.

I also believe that another consideration that can help improve your sleep is knowing that you have put in a good day's work, that you haven't done anything to be hurtful to anyone else, and that perhaps what you did today helped someone else. People who feel good about what they have done are able to sleep in way that is restful to the body and spirit.

THE TOXIC

Embracing the good is not sufficient to put a person on the path to stability and joy. You also have to step back and refrain from the toxic. Very often, the most toxic things present themselves in ways that have immediate appeal. Toxic food can taste delicious and overwhelm our judgment, like processed foods that are heavy in sweeteners, salt, and chemicals that are used specifically to get us to overindulge. In regard to relationships, some people use their charms to manipulate others and get what they want. Toxic things may appear harmless, but they are often addictive and not good for us. The elimination of toxic things needs to be approached in a straightforward manner in order to keep you on the right track.

The most difficult aspect about toxic things is that they usually start out in a relatively benign way, but over time, they completely consume the individual. Their embrace never releases its grip, clinging to us until we are powerless and emotionally suffocated. People in toxic situations are on the path to depression and other health issues.

Given the way life is, the greatest challenge is to refrain from the toxic. You cannot eliminate all that is toxic from your life—for instance, the mother-in-law that you visit but never exchanges a kind word with you or the supervisor who is never satisfied with what you do. "Refrain from the toxic" means you have to learn to step back when necessary. If you engage with the toxic, it can consume you. These changes will take significant effort, but you need to refrain from the toxic in order to avoid depression.

Toxic Stress

Life had become very complicated since Yolanda had been asked to take on new responsibilities at work. Everything at home was the same. Yolanda woke up every morning and prepared breakfast for the family, did house chores, left for work, worked a full day, and hurried home in time to make dinner that was not too late. After dinner she would clean up and get ready for the next day. The day never seemed long enough to get everything done. Yolanda was starting to feel that the stress was getting to her. Trying to do everything she would always do was starting to get to her in a way she could not understand. In the past it seemed she always enjoyed the stress that came from her work.

When life changes, we need to alter the ways we do things as well. Yolanda took on new responsibilities but did not make any adjustments to her day. While some stress is good, too much stress will be detrimental to you in every way. The major problem here is that some people do not know how to assess how much stress they have. So as the level of stress slowly increases, a person just endures it until it eventually becomes too much to handle.

You need to recognize your acceptable stress level, your tolerable stress level, and your danger zone. When your stress reaches the tolerable level, you need to dial the situation back. While you may not be able to completely control the situation, you can make yourself step back from it. In Yolanda's case, she was approaching the danger zone and needed to ask the other members of her household to step up to the plate to help her.

The ways we handle stress ranges somewhere along the parameters of "fight or flight" or "to tend and befriend." For many years, fight or flight was the only explanation about how people handled stress. Specifically, when you received stress signals, your body would prepare you either to stay to fight or to flee to get out of the situation. Most of these data were based on studies of men. Later research documented that women facing stress generally use the strategy of "to tend and befriend" instead of "fight or flight." According to these findings, when women are under stress, they rely on their social networks for support. Now we know that men also have tend/befriend behaviors. Recent research suggests that women prefer to tend, befriend, and flight responses, while men engage in more fight responses than women.[71] Men and women do not necessarily have two different strategies in response to stress. In fact, it is more likely that each individual's response to stressful events is guided by the situation. If someone is about to get physically attacked, then "tend and befriend" certainly would not be in the person's best interest. No matter what strategy someone decides to follow, the reality is that when you experience an increase in stress, your body will continue to produce more cortisol. And that is not good because rising cortisol levels makes it more difficult for your immune cells to function properly.

All of us have some stress in our lives, and up to a certain point stress is good: it serves as a motivator and helps us keep our senses sharp. However, allowing stress to build by simply coping with it is not as helpful as it sounds. Researchers in the field of social genomics have confirmed that chronic adversity, such as stress, affects your immune system at the molecular level. Stress makes the body release chemicals in the brain that create problems for the person.

Toxic Relationships

The primary relationship you have is with yourself. Your self-image is what drives your self-esteem. While there is always room for improvement, begin by not dwelling on negative statements about yourself. Sure, you have made mistakes, but focusing on them does not help you. Learn lessons from your mistakes and drop any negative thoughts that make you feel that you are less than you are. In order to stay healthy, you have to celebrate yourself even with your flaws.

But how do you know that a relationship is toxic? There are some boundaries that place a relationship in the toxic zone: abuse of any kind (physical, emotional, or sexual) is unacceptable. People who are abusers tend to be manipulative. Like a vampire seeking a new victim, abusers know how to put on a good front in order to attract the next person that they have selected as their prey. Abusers are keenly attuned to their victims' vulnerabilities and use those vulnerabilities to keep them where they want them. This occurs whether the abuser is a man or woman.

> *It was hard to be Leonor's friend—she was always negative and grumpy. For her, the glass was not only half full but it was also leaking. I wanted to be her friend but could only take her a little bit at time. Her negativity was totally exhausting.*

Toxic relationships are the ones that are draining. There is no sharing of positive experiences: you keep giving and giving and the other person does not reciprocate. You are not necessarily expecting an even exchange or keeping an emotional ledger; you just feel like the person is sucking energy out of your life. Take the person who is always needy or negative: they know how to latch on to a kind, giving person in a way that will meet their goals. Although their neediness can be subtle and not overtly demanding, it is still incredibly depleting.

To an outside observer, it would seem that walking away from a toxic relationship should be easy. But it is not easy. Toxic relationships often become more difficult to escape from as the toxic person learns to lean into you. They know how to manipulate the situation so that it is difficult to leave.

We mistakenly believe that by focusing our time and energy on these unhealthy relationships and giving them the attention that they want, the person will get better. But why should that happen if they are getting what they want? If their manipulative strategies appear to work, they will have no desire to change. Only people who want to change do change. Regardless of the toxic individual's demands, they will always be emotionally draining.

Unhealthy relationships are more demanding and less rewarding than healthy ones. If you want to save yourself, sometimes you have to walk away. In situations where you cannot leave, the solution is to set limits on others' invasiveness and change the ways you interact with them. It is essential to establish healthy boundaries, and to protect yourself, sometimes you have to say no.

Food

While some consider food to be the enemy, the reality is that food is essential for life. You cannot give up food; you just have to consider why you eat, what you eat, and how you eat. When you eat without thinking, you will not give your body the fuel it needs to function well and, as a result, you will not be as healthy as you could be

Not all food is good for you, and too much food prevents your body from working well. In order to eat food that is best for you, you should avoid processed foods. A 2009 study found that at the end of five years, the group that ate more processed food was more prone to depression than those who ate more whole food. [72]

Alcohol

> "*Beer is a symbol of celebration, of refuge, it's something to cure depression, to have at a party, a wedding, to drink at home*" *Luis Alberto Medina, host of a radio show in the Northern City of Hermosillo.*[73]

Alcohol is <u>not</u> a cure for depression. Unfortunately, Mr. Medina reflects a commonly held but incorrect belief about the relationship between alcohol and depression. Not only is alcohol <u>not</u> a cure but people who have depression are at risk of developing an alcohol use disorder. What may begin as a seemingly harmless way to self-medicate can end with disastrous consequences. In 2018, 26.45 percent of people ages 18 or older reported that they engaged in binge drinking in the past month, and 6.6 percent reported that they engaged in heavy alcohol use in the past month.[74] Alcohol use is pervasive.

Alcohol interferes with the brain's communication pathways and can affect the way the brain works. These disruptions can change one's mood and behavior, making it harder to think clearly and move with coordination.[75] It is also crucial to keep in mind that alcohol is a toxic substance. In 2020, the American Cancer Society changed their earlier permissive recommendations to "it is best not to drink alcohol."[76]

One drink is a lot less than most people think, and many people have to be reminded that beer is alcohol. A 12-ounce bottle of beer, a 5-ounce glass of wine, or 1 ½-ounces (shot) of hard liquor are equal to one drink. Additionally, when you order a "specialty drink," there are two or three different shots in one glass. So your one glass may actually be two or three drinks.

In general, excessive or heavy alcohol use is:

- Men who have 15 or more drinks a week.
- Women who have 7 or more drinks a week.

Binge drinking occurs when women have 4 or more drinks or men have 5 or more drinks in about 2 hours. Binge drinking may indicate a vulnerability to alcohol use disorder.

If you are depressed, alcohol use can lead to alcohol abuse and dependence, making depression more difficult to treat in the long run.

Tobacco is Toxic

Remember that nicotine is a highly addictive chemical compound present in the tobacco plant and that tobacco products are designed to get you addicted. It is not a way to manage depression. Tobacco smoke is made up of thousands of chemicals, including at least 70 known to cause cancer.

When you inhale smoke from a cigarette (regardless of whether you or someone else is smoking) those toxins enter your body through your lungs and are picked up by red blood cells that need oxygen. Those red blood cells then transport the toxic substance to every cell in your body. Smoking and even being around smokers is bad because it introduces a toxic chemical to each cell in your body. Smoking not only interferes with the effectiveness of some medications, but it is also very unattractive and even repugnant to some. Keep in mind the old saying, "Kissing a smoker is like licking an ashtray."

Smokeless tobacco or chewing tobacco is also toxic. According to the Centers for Disease Control and Prevention smokeless tobacco can lead to nicotine addiction; causes cancer of the mouth, esophagus, and pancreas; and, can increase risks for early delivery and stillbirth when used during pregnancy.

Marijuana and Other Substances

Whether or not they are legal, these substances interfere with how your brain works and are not a treatment for depression. We are just starting to document the ways these substances play a critical role in disrupting the brain. Some of these substances may trigger the changes in the brain that lead to or worsen depression.[77]

THE WAVES

I work so hard at keeping myself afloat. I embrace the good, I refrain from the toxic and still what I see is wave after wave. I just want to be in the calm water.

Life is about the waves. To manage your life and stay afloat, you need to learn to enjoy the waves. Before you know it, you will be able to achieve this…and you may even learn how to surf.

The devastating effects of COVID-19 taught us all how unpredictable life could be. In a moment, our life changed from going to group activities to having to stay home and not having contact with others. During that time, countless people experienced great sadness. Many people were alone, and for some the silence of solitude was unbearable. The uncertainty of what would happen next, the lack of income, and the need to depend on others changed us forever. We collectively learned that we may not have liked the changes, but we did learn to adapt to them.

To survive we had to make the disruption in our lives be transformative. The waves are part of life.

MOVING FORWARD

When you feel yourself getting pulled in the wrong direction—and you will have those moments again—you need to pause and recognize what you are doing. It is natural to slip up every now and then, but in order to understand how you feel and monitor your depression, you need to regain your focus and get back on the program.

Examine what you are currently doing, what you still need to do, and where you are going. If you make corrections as the situation changes, you will manage your life in a way that decreases the likelihood of depression. You need to focus on the things you tell yourself you have to do. This is not about making lists of things that will never get done, but, rather, acknowledging that you must address the various elements that make up life in order to truly enjoy it.

The ways you experience depression vary depending on your personal history, triggering events, and the resources you have at hand. Your response when you or someone you know is depressed can make all the difference between getting better or sinking more deeply into depression.

In order to manage your depression, it is important to understand what you have to do and not allow your mind to wander to unpleasant or negative thoughts. You need to stay focused in the present in order to get to a better place. In the past, researchers believed that sadness made people's minds wander. Recent research has documented that the reverse actually happens—when your mind wanders, you become unhappy. Staying focused is good.

You also have to discard some common ideas about what depression is, who has depression, and how to manage it. To move forward, you need to know and accept that there are actions that you can take to reduce your risk of depression, and that there is treatment for it. The key things for you to remember are simple, as they are the basics for healthy living for you and your family.

As challenging as it may be, you must make yourself do what will improve your mental health and well-being. You have to be more thoughtful about your life and reorganize yourself for wellness. You will have to rethink how you spend your time and all of your resources. Most importantly, the three self-statements that need to frame your daily life are: (1) embrace the good, (2) refrain from the toxic, and (3) enjoy the waves.

There certainly is no solution that will work in all instances and seeking professional support, treatment, and guidance may be an excellent next step. And remember that you deserve to be happy and to enjoy life.

OPTIONS FOR TREATMENT FOR DEPRESSION

When you want to know the facts, you ask people you trust and search for answers on the internet. There is so much information online that it takes a long time to go through it all and find what is useful. There is also a lot of hype and misinformation on the internet. This section, listed in alphabetical order, is a synthesis of available information for some of the most common forms of treatment and approaches. There is no "one-size-fits-all" approach to treatment; it may take some trial and error to find the treatment that works best for you. The good news is that once you do so, you will get better.

BRAIN STIMULATION THERAPY

These are very serious procedures that are typically reserved only for people with severe, major depression that is very disabling. This treatment specifically targets people for whom no other treatments have worked. There are several types of therapies that fall in this category: electroconvulsive therapy (also known as ECT or shock therapy), vagus nerve stimulation, repetitive transcranial magnetic stimulation, magnetic seizure therapy, and deep brain stimulation. In these treatments, the brain is stimulated by activating or touching the brain with magnets, implants, or an electrical current, as outlined below.[78]

Electroconvulsive Therapy (ECT)

According to the National Institute of Mental Health, "This type of therapy is usually considered only if a patient's illness has not improved after other treatments (such as antidepressant medication or psychotherapy) are tried, or in cases where rapid response is needed (as in the case of suicide risk and catatonia, for example)."

During the procedure, the person is sedated with general anesthesia and given a muscle relaxant so that they do not move in the process. Electrodes are placed at precise locations on the head. Several short bursts of electricity are directed to the electrodes to induce a brain seizure that lasts less than a minute. People undergoing ECT feel neither pain nor the electrical impulses because of the sedation and relaxants that they received. After about 10 minutes, the person awakens and will feel better as the anesthesia wears off. It is typical that after an hour, the person is alert and can resume their activities. In most cases, people undergo this treatment three times a week for up to 12 sessions to lift their depression. In this procedure, the electrical current causes changes in the brain chemistry that are believed to stabilize depression.

Vagus Nerve Stimulation (VNS)

The vagus nerve carries signals and messages from the part of your brain that controls mood, sleep, and other functions to your heart, lungs, liver, and stomach. In VNS, a person undergoes surgery to have a device similar to a pacemaker implanted under the skin in the upper left side of the chest. A wire is guided under the skin from the device to the vagus nerve. The device is programmed to send electrical impulses through the left vagus nerve on a set schedule. Although this was developed as a treatment for epilepsy in 2005, the FDA approved its use for major depression under the following specific conditions, as follows:

- if the patient is 18 years of age or over; and
- if the illness has lasted two years or more; and
- if it is severe or recurrent; and,
- if the depression has not eased after trying at least four other treatments.

The findings on this type of treatment are mixed. The best results were in a 2013 study which found that 32 percent of depressed people responded to VSN and 14 percent had full remission of symptoms after being treated for nearly two years.[79]

According to NIMH, "VNS should only be prescribed and monitored by doctors who have specific training and expertise in the management of treatment-resistant depression and the use of this device."

Repetitive Transcranial Magnetic Stimulation (rTMS)

In this procedure, a magnet is used to activate a specific site in the brain. While a particular region of the brain can be targeted to minimize any other impacts on the brain, opinions differ as to which location is the optimal site. An electromagnetic coil is held against the forehead near an area of the brain that is thought to be involved in mood regulation. The treatment lasts 30 to 60 minutes and does not require anesthesia.

The FDA permitted marketing of TMS as a treatment for major depression in 2008, treating pain associated with certain migraine headaches in 2013, and obsessive-compulsive disorders (OCD) in 2018.[80]

Magnetic Seizure Therapy (MST)

This procedure, which requires general anesthesia, uses a very strong magnetic pulse on a specific area of the brain to induce a seizure. The best available research suggests that 30 to 40 percent of people with major depression or bipolar disorder experienced remission after MST.[81]

Deep Brain Stimulation (DBS)

In DBS, electrodes implanted in your brain are connected to lead wires attached to a device that is implanted in your chest. This procedure involves brain surgery and has all of its associated risks. It was initially developed as a means to control the tremors and uncontrollable movements that characterize those with Parkinson's disease. According to NIMH, " . . . its use in depression remains only on an experimental basis."

Useful? It depends. Some of these treatments have benefited people with difficult-to-treat depression.

Concerns? Long term effects are still under investigation. Given the invasiveness of some of these procedures, the problems encountered are ones that arise from general anesthesia, major surgery, and implants. There is a considerable amount of research that needs to be done to understand how they work as well as any long-term effects. For example, with rTMS, the exact location to direct the electromagnetic stimulation is still under discussion. And while there has been much progress in the delivery of ECT since 1938, when it was first introduced, there is still controversy around the way it works and its effects on memory.

CLINICAL TRIALS

Although clinical trials are not a form of treatment, they provide ways for some to gain access to treatment. A clinical trial is a biomedical or health-related research study that has specific criteria as to who will be allowed to participate in the research study, the types of treatments that will be offered, and all of the details of what will happen during and after the study.

Each study is designed to answer specific questions, which is why researchers carefully describe the characteristics you have to meet to be in the study (inclusion criteria) and those that exclude you from participation (exclusion criteria). Examples of these types of criteria include age, gender, the type and severity of a disease, previous treatment history, and other medical conditions.

Useful? Clinical trials are the only way to determine the effectiveness of a treatment.

Concerns? One of the key concerns is obtaining informed consent from all participants in a clinical trial. Before agreeing to be a participant, you need to understand all aspects of what you have agreed to do. You and all other prospective participants must receive a written document that includes details about the purpose of the study, how long the study will last, required procedures, risks and potential benefits, and key contacts. The document should be in the language you understand. After you have read the document and have had any questions answered, you can then decide whether or not to sign the document. Keep in mind that the informed consent document is not a contract; you can withdraw from a clinical trial at any time.

COGNITIVE BEHAVIORAL THERAPY (CBT)

In this type of therapy, a person learns to think about previously known facts in new ways (cognitive restructuring) and apply this new way of thinking to what they do (behavior). Both the therapist and the person are actively engaged in this process. The therapist helps the person sort through the facts, identify when his or her thoughts do not match the facts, and how his or her behavior needs to be consistent with what he or she now knows. In some cases, CBT encourages the person to identify what is triggering the depression and to make necessary changes.

This type of therapy works to help you sort through your thoughts so that you can achieve the things you want to do. It also helps you analyze and stop having thoughts and beliefs that produce maladaptive and unhealthy behaviors.

Useful? CBT alone is very effective for people with minor to moderate depression. Some people may need a combination of CBT and medication.

Concerns? No. Lots of evidence supporting its effectiveness with depression. For CBT to be effective, you must be able to talk honestly about what is going on in your life and be willing to make changes.

COMPLEMENTARY, ALTERNATIVE, FUNCTIONAL, OR INTEGRATIVE MEDICINE

The National Center for Complementary and Integrative Health (NCCIH) is part of the National Institutes of Health. The mission of NCCIH is to define, through rigorous scientific investigation, the usefulness and safety of complementary and integrative health interventions and their roles in improving health and health care.

According to a 2012 national survey, many Americans— more than 30 percent of adults—use health care approaches that are not typically part of conventional medical care or that may have origins outside of usual Western practice. Here are some key terms to better understand these forms of medicine:

Complementary Medicine: conventional medicine plus non-mainstream practice. Complementary health approaches include natural products and mind and body practices.

Alternative Medicine: a non-mainstream practice that is used in place of conventional medicine.

Integrative Medicine: a combination of conventional and complementary approaches in a coordinated way. It emphasizes a holistic, patient-focused approach to health care and wellness— often including mental, emotional, functional, spiritual, social, and community aspects—and treating the whole person rather than, for example, one organ system.

NCCIH states that some complementary approaches, such as the practices of traditional healers, ayurvedic medicine, traditional Chinese medicine, homeopathy, naturopathy, and functional medicine, may not perfectly fit into any of the above groups.

Useful? There is great variability in the degree of success for each of the above approached. There is evidence that acupuncture, music therapy, and yoga all provide some level of relief with respect to depression.

Concerns? The popular media often tout these, even in cases where evidence-based medicine has not proven their effectiveness. A greater concern is that a person's limited health care dollars will be wasted on products that do not deliver what they promise.

INTERPERSONAL THERAPY (IPT)

This treatment is based on the belief that one's interactions with others play a major role in depression. This therapy works to improve communication and the way people relate to each other. It is less focused on thoughts and places more emphasis on relationships and interpersonal dynamics.

This treatment is considered short term because it takes place in 12 to 16 weekly one-hour sessions that focus on one or two problems. It is a highly structured intervention with three phases: a beginning (one to three sessions), middle, and end (three sessions). Once a person is diagnosed with depression, the problem is related to one of four areas: grieving, impasse in a relationship, getting through a major life transition (divorce or retirement), or having negative interpersonal behaviors. Sessions with a mental health professional involve talking about what is going on in your current life and developing skills and strategies to improve your life situation. For example, if your relationship is at an impasse, you are first tasked with deciding whether or not to end it. Once that decision is made, subsequent sessions focus on the actions you can take to move the relationship in the right direction. If the depression is in response to the death of a loved one, initial sessions focus on allowing the person to grieve, while later sessions address how to introduce new activities and relationships into the mourner's life to ease their loss.

Sometimes, the therapist will work to identify painful trigger events from the past before guiding the person so that they can express their lingering emotions in a healthy way.

Poor relationships from the past are analyzed by identifying the distorted thinking that led to those problems so that a person can gain a more objective view of their current relationships.

Useful? ITP is usually used to treat depression and has been shown to be effective.[82] This effectiveness included a telephone-based intervention for postpartum depression.[83]

Concerns? Some professionals view ITP as too limited in its duration and its focus. According to the International Society for Interpersonal Psychotherapy, IPT "addresses interpersonal issues in depression to the exclusion of all other foci of clinical attention."

LIGHT THERAPY

Light therapy is also known as bright light therapy or phototherapy. We know that when light reaches the brain it can alter brain centers that regulate circadian (body clock) timing, sleep, and mood. Specific properties of light, such as intensity, wavelength, and timing, are key to understanding individual differences in light sensitivity.

In this type of therapy, a person is exposed to a light box that emits artificial light for a specific span of time in the morning, usually when it is still quite dark outdoors. The light produced is at the full spectrum with the intent of replacing the diminished sunlight of the fall and winter months and should be designed to filter out harmful ultraviolet (UV) light.

You have to sit by the light box while you read, write, or eat. The light box should be about 16 to 24 inches (41 to 61 centimeters) from your face. You should not look directly at the light. The length of time you have to sit is a function of the amount of light coming from the light box. A 10,000-lux illumination may require only 30 minutes of exposure, while a 2,500-lux may require two hours. These boxes are available for purchase online and at local drug stores.

Useful? Since the 1980s, this has been documented to be an effective treatment for people with seasonal affective disorder (SAD). Recent evidence from the first study of studies on the effectiveness of light therapy found it to be effective for the treatment of depression.[84]

Concerns? The person has to commit to exposing themselves to the amount of light on a regular schedule.

MEDICATION

Henry had no idea how the medication would help him. His entire life, he had felt as if he were drowning in feelings of depression. He had managed to be successful because people only saw him for short periods. At the suggestion of his internist, Henry decided to try some medication. He reluctantly started to take his medication and after a few weeks he could feel that something was different. The medication did not make him feel happy. What he felt was very unusual. For the first time, rather than going deeper into his depression, he felt as if something were lifting his chin out of the water and holding it up. These pills did not make him happy, but they did give him added support so that he did not feel as if he were drowning. He could look up and see that there was an alternative to being inundated in his own despair.

Medications for depression are formulated to improve the chemistry in the brain. As of now, there is no way to determine which medication will work best for a particular person and produce the fewest side effects.

Depression may be treated with medicines, such as selective serotonin reuptake inhibitors (SSRIs), serotonin and norepinephrine reuptake inhibitors (SNRIs), or norepinephrine and dopamine reuptake inhibitors (NDRIs). For decades, SSRI's were the first choice for treating depression.[85] Today, SNRI's are more commonly prescribed because they have fewer side effects. The generic forms of these medications are listed below with the brand name in parentheses.

SSRIs: citalopram (Celexa), escitalopram (Lexapro), fluoxetine (Prozac), fluvoxamine (Luvox), paroxetine (Paxil), and sertraline (Zoloft). Some similar drugs include: vilazodone (Viibryd) and vortioxetine (Trintellix formerly called Brintellix).

SNRIs: duloxetine (Cymbalta), venlafaxine (Effexor), desvenlafaxine ER (Khedezla), levomilnacipran (Fetzima), and desvenlafaxine (Pristiq).

NDRIs: bupropion (Wellbutrin)

Recently, the U.S. Food and Drug Administration (FDA) approved two new antidepressants, esketamine and brexanolone. These are not medications that you take on your own. Esketamine appears to have immediate effects with treatment-resistant depression and helps by muting ideas of suicide.[86] Esketamine must be administered under the direct supervision of a health care provider and the person typically has to stay in the office for observation for 2 hours. Brexanolone is used for postpartum depression. Its approval status limits its delivery to certain certified health care facilities and requires a patient to be hospitalized for 60 hours. Its cost is also a concern.[87]

Differences in the ways people respond to medication can also be a function of age, the speed at which their body uses a drug, how consistently they take their medication, and other factors. For example, there is strong evidence that smoking impacts the ways your body is able to use the medicines you take.

Once you start taking a psychotropic medication (that is, medicine designed to have an effect on the mind and address conditions such as depression), you need to speak with your health care provider if you want to stop taking it.

When you are prescribed medications for depression, make sure to ask and write down the answers to these key questions:

1. What is the name of the medication that you want me to take?
2. How much will I be taking?
3. When do I take it?
4. Are there any special instructions about how to take it?
5. How long will I have to take it?
6. How long will it be before it starts to work?
7. What happens if I forget to take it?
8. Are there any side effects that I should be concerned about?
9. How often will I see you about my medication?
10. Are there any interactions with the other medicines, supplements, teas, and over-the-counter products I am taking?

Useful? According to the National Institute of Mental Health (NIMH), medication is most useful for someone who has moderate to severe depression, as determined by a health care provider. Medication and psychotherapy combined provide the best outcomes. While there is no such thing as a "happy pill," you can manage your depression if you take the medication that is best for you.

It usually takes two to four weeks of consistent use to know whether or not a medicine works for you. If one medicine does not work, then your health care provider may recommend a different one. Usually, when people need to change medications, they are able to find one that will work for them.

Concerns? Older medications, such as tricyclics and monoamine oxidase inhibitors (MAOIs), can have serious side effects and are usually avoided. To maximize the benefits of your medication, you should also be involved in psychotherapy. Side effects are always a concern, and an ongoing problem is that some people do not take their medicines as consistently as they should.

PSYCHOANALYTIC THERAPY

This may be the most well-known type of therapy, but it is the least used today as a treatment for mental illness or mental health problems. This type of treatment, also known as psychoanalysis, is based on the work of Sigmund Freud. The sessions involve talking about how the unconscious mind influences what people are experiencing today. Considerable time and effort are also spent to uncover how childhood experiences contribute to current problems. As part of the treatment, the therapist may use techniques such as free association, dream interpretation, and role-playing. Treatment typically requires sessions at least once a week for several years.

Useful? Comparative studies have documented that psychoanalysis is no more effective than a placebo.

Concerns? The long-term cost of psychoanalysis, as well as the intensive form of treatment involved in this approach, may make it less appealing to most people.

PSYCHODYNAMIC THERAPY

Although this therapy was originally based in the theories of Sigmund Freud, it has changed its focus over the years toward helping people gain greater self-awareness and understanding of their own actions. Some psychodynamic therapists use a combination, or eclectic, approach to treatment that includes other more behaviorally-oriented therapy. It is both shorter in duration and less intense than psychoanalytic therapy and requires active involvement by the therapist.

Useful? It all depends on the skill of your therapist.

Concerns? According to the National Institute of Mental Health (NIMH), research into the effectiveness of this type of therapy has garnered mixed results.

PSYCHOTHERAPY (TALK THERAPY)

Psychotherapy is the term given to all of the treatments for mental health conditions that involve talking to a mental health professional. In this type of treatment, people are encouraged to talk about their feelings and their life situation to gain an understanding of their situation. In most instances, the first few sessions are spent obtaining information about the person's life and the concerns she or he has. Based on their discussions, the therapist develops a treatment plan to meet the person's needs. Depending on the diagnosis, medication may also be part of the treatment plan.

At the core of psychotherapy is the relationship between the person and the mental health professional. This is a major factor in the effectiveness of the treatment.

When I was first training to be a clinical psychologist, I watched my professor perform psychotherapy and commented that it seemed like he was just talking. He smiled, thanked me, and added that when you are really good at psychotherapy, it looks like a regular conversation. In the decades that I have seen individuals, couples, and families, I have grown to appreciate that wisdom.

Psychotherapy is hard work for both the mental health professional and the person in therapy. The mental health professional needs to listen, process, and respond instantly to what is being said. The individual has to be honest, be willing to discuss difficult topics, be vulnerable, listen, and use what he or she discusses to take the necessary steps in their life. Psychotherapy is not about having a one-hour session and feeling good afterwards. It is about the work you do when you are not in the session.

Useful? Yes. There are different types of psychotherapy that are effective for specific problems. Both cognitive behavioral therapy and IPT have worked well with people who are diagnosed with depression.

Concerns? It is essential that a person be as honest as she or he can be when talking to their mental health professional.

SUPPLEMENTS

Dietary supplements are vitamin and mineral products, botanical or herbal products, amino acid products, or enzyme supplements that you can buy without a prescription. Supplements are not intended to treat, diagnose, cure, or alleviate the effects of diseases. You should you speak with your health care professional *before* using any dietary supplement, especially if you are taking other medications.

 Currently, federal law does not require dietary supplements to be approved by the FDA. Keep an eye out for the USP Verified Mark, as shown here. This mark indicates that the product (1) contains the ingredients listed on the label in the declared potency and amounts, (2) does not contain harmful levels of specified contaminants, (3) has been made according to the FDA's current Good Manufacturing Practices using sanitary and well-controlled procedures, and (4) will break down and release into the body within a specified amount of time.

Information regarding the use of supplements continues to evolve.

Useful? According to NIMH and NCCIH, other natural products sold as dietary supplements, including St. John's wort (*Hypericum perforatum*), omega-3 fatty acid, inositol, and S-adenosylmethionine (SAMe), remain under study but have not yet been proven safe and effective for routine use.[88,89]

Concerns? There are serious concerns about how St. John's wort (*Hypericum perforatum*), a top-selling botanical product, limits the effectiveness of many prescription medicines.

RESOURCES AND TOOLS

I f you have questions about depression, please call the National Hispanic Family Health Help Line at 866-783-2645 or 866-SU-FAMILIA. Health promotion advisors are available to answer your questions in English and Spanish and to help you find local services. You can call Monday through Friday, from 9 a.m. to 6 p.m. ET.

WEBSITES AND HELPLINES

Noncommercial websites

Alianza Nacional para la Salud Hispana	nuestrasalud.org
National Alliance for Hispanic Health	healthyamericas.org
National Institute of Mental Health (NIMH)	nimh.nih.gov
National Institute of Neurological Disorders and Stroke	ninds.nih.gov
National Library of Medicine (NLM): MedlinePlus	nlm.nih.gov
National Center for Complementary and Integrative Health	nccih.nih.gov

24/7 Crisis Hotlines

National Suicide Prevention Lifeline 1-800-273-TALK (8255)

En Español 1-888-628-9454

Connects callers to the nearest crisis center in their network of centers that provide crisis counseling and mental health referrals.

Crisis Text Line: Text "HELLO" to 741741

Connects callers to a crisis counselor who can provide support and information.

Veterans Crisis Line 1-800-273-TALK (8255) and press 1 or text to 838255

This service is available to all veterans, even if they are not registered with the VA or enrolled in VA health care.

Disaster Distress Helpline: 1-800-985-5990 or text "TalkWithUs" to 66746

The disaster distress helpline provides immediate crisis counseling for people who are experiencing emotional distress related to any natural or human-caused disaster.

HOW TO SELECT A MENTAL HEALTH PROFESSIONAL

When you decide to seek support, begin by speaking with your health care provider to rule out any physical conditions. Your primary health care provider (PCP) may be a physician, nurse practitioner, or physician assistant. These are some questions that you can ask your health care provider to better understand your options.

Make sure to write down the answers. It is clear that when we are with our health care providers, our memory is not at its best. If you cannot write down the necessary information yourself, then have someone go with you when you have the conversation with your health care provider and take notes for you.

Questions About Your Options

1. Do you think I am depressed?
2. Should I see a mental health professional?
3. Do you have any recommendations for a mental health professional?
4. Is there anything else that I should do?
5. Is there medication that I can take?
6. What are the side effects of this medication?
7. How long will I have to take this medication?
8. Are there any alternatives to taking medication?
9. Do you have any other recommendations?

There are many different kinds of mental health professionals. Some are licensed with specific requirements that vary by state, and some are not licensed. Here are some of the major types of mental health professionals with a short description of their training and what they can do. The type of psychotherapy that mental health professionals provide is based on the approach they choose to follow. The list below is in alphabetical order.

1. *Licensed professional counselors* earn a master's degree (MA) in psychology, counseling, or a similar discipline and typically have at least two years of postgraduate experience. They may provide services that include diagnosis and counseling (individual, family/group, or both).

2. *Psychiatric/mental health nurses* may have degrees ranging from associate to doctoral level (DNSc, DSN, PhD). Depending on their education and licensing, they provide a broad range of services, including assessment, case management, and psychotherapy. In certain states, some psychiatric nurses may prescribe and monitor medication.

3. *Psychiatrists* are physicians who have an MD or OD degree and have at least four more years of specialized study and training in psychiatry. Psychiatrists are licensed as physicians to practice medicine by individual states. "Board-certified" psychiatrists have passed the national examination administered by the American Board of Psychiatry and Neurology. Psychiatrists provide medical and psychiatric evaluations, offer psychotherapy, and prescribe and monitor medications.

4. *Psychologists* include people who have a master's degree (MA or MS) in psychology; a doctoral degree (PhD) in clinical, counseling, or research psychology; a doctorate in psychology that focuses on applied work (PsyD); or a doctorate in education (EdD). Most states have licensing requirements for people to practice psychology; these require psychologists to pass national and state exams. A psychologist is licensed to administer psychological tests, conduct evaluations, and provide psychotherapy. Psychologists may prescribe and monitor medication in Iowa, Idaho, Illinois, Louisiana, and New Mexico as well as in the Public Health Service, the Indian Health Service, the U.S. military, and Guam.

5. *Psychopharmacologists* are usually psychiatrists who specialize in the use of psychiatric drugs to manage mental disorders.

6. *Social workers* may have a bachelor's degree, a master's degree (MSW), or a doctoral degree (DSW or PhD). Most states license social workers after they pass an examination to be licensed to practice social work (LCSW). Social workers provide various services, including case management, hospital discharge planning, and psychotherapy.

When you take the step to see a mental health professional, ask for recommendations from your health care provider and people you trust. Your final choice will be based on how well the two of you communicate with each other, as well as the affordability of the services.

Before making an appointment, call the office and obtain some basic information about the person and the practice. Specifically:

License. Make sure you know the type of mental health professional you are consulting and that he or she is licensed. If a person is licensed, they completed educational requirements from an accredited institution, met your state's standards for the profession, agreed to follow and be held to a code of ethical conduct, and earns continuing education credits on an ongoing basis. Although required licenses vary by state, I strongly recommend that, when you are looking for a mental health professional, she or he be licensed. It is troubling that in most states, anyone can claim to be a psychotherapist or therapist or counselor without having any type of formal training or standardized license.

Language. Make sure the person speaks your language. This does not mean that you can pick someone just because he or she has a familiar last name. If you are looking for a language-specific mental health professional, be sure to ask for this option before you schedule a visit.

Hours of Operation. Their hours need to match your availability based on your flexibility during the day.

Fees. You need to know what it will cost for the first visit and for future sessions. Some providers work on a scale that is based on your income. In other practices, the fee for the first visit may be waived and the session may be shorter than the typical 45-to-50 minute session. It is also good to know about any of the following that may be important to you:

1. What type of insurance is accepted? Medicare? Medicaid?
2. Does the practice accept direct billing to or payment from your insurance company?
3. Is there a sliding-scale fee policy?
4. Does the practice accept credit cards?
5. Are telehealth visits included?

During your first visit, your interaction with the person should make you feel that they value you and your culture. You should ask about the person's success with similar issues, as well as how long people who were successfully treated had to stay in therapy.

Most importantly, be aware of how well the person listens to what you have to say. In most types of psychotherapy, the relationship you have with your mental health professional will be key to your progress. Your ability to feel comfortable with him or her is essential. If you feel that you cannot reveal your feelings or experiences with him or her, then you should see someone else.

TELEHEALTH

Lori Gottlieb's recent article "The surprising intimacy of online therapy sessions"[90] in the *Washington Post* documents that we are at a new beginning. We are leveraging the benefits of teletherapy and virtual care while maintaining the core value of human connectedness.

COVID-19 opened the door to the broad acceptance of telehealth, as people needed to connect with their health care provider while simultaneously staying home. The explosive numbers for Partners Healthcare tell the story of the rise of telehealth in Massachusetts. In 2020 televisits for Partners in Healthcare increased from 1,600 visits in February to 89,000 in March to 242,000 in April.[91] The demand was enormous, since televisits allowed people who were getting sick to see a health care provider from the comfort of their home.

Demand for health care services was constant, but it had to be provided outside of the customary office visit. This demand put booster rockets on the implementation of the Primer on Implementing Telehealth for Obstetrician-Gynecologist that the American College of Obstetrics and Gynecologists had released in January 2020. It also made the Physicians Foundation, American Medical Association, Florida Medical Association, Massachusetts Medical Society and Texas Medical Association joint Telehealth Initiative launch in March. This was earlier than was originally planned, as physicians needed guidance and help to implement telehealth services. Soon afterwards, the American Medical Association (AMA) put out its 128-page Digital Health Implementation Playbook Series. Around the same time, the American Academy of Pediatrics released their guidance. NIMH also indicated that "While the technology frontier offers promising opportunities for mental health care, much work remains to address questions about efficacy and effectiveness, regulation, and privacy."[92] The time for telehealth had come.

The mental health community had already been moving in this direction and was helped along by Michael Phelps, the American swimmer and most decorated Olympian of all time, with a total of 28 medals. Phelps' struggles with depression led him to become a mental health advocate. His goal was to reduce the stigma that prevents people from talking about their condition and seeking help. Based on his success and the changes he experienced in therapy in 2018, he became a spokesperson for Talkspace.

Talkspace describes itself as "…the most convenient and affordable way to connect with a licensed therapist — all from the privacy of your device. Send your therapist text, audio, picture, and video messages at any time, and they will respond daily, 5x/week. If you're looking for the "face-to-face" therapy experience, we also offer Live Video Sessions so you and your therapist can plan to connect in real-time." This was a huge shift for the provision of mental health services.

In 2020, mental health visits became increasingly online-based when APA's Psychologist Locator added a telehealth filter. Each person could get some level of treatment when and where they wanted it. And since many of these options were developed to accommodate peoples' need to stay home, health care became much more accessible to others.

The genie had been let out of the bottle and it was not going back. Telehealth was no longer available just to those with Concierge services or to those who were at the other extreme and had no other way to access health care. Telehealth was now designed to meet the person when and where they were.

With telehealth, many more people will now be able to access the care they need. Given your situation, this may be a way for you to access the care you need.

FROM MY HEART TO YOURS

I wrote this book because I do not want anyone to suffer needlessly. It does not matter whether you are dealing with your own depression or someone else's. What matters is the action you take. And doing something different is tough, even when it is something you want to do.

There are many people who have endured life with ongoing depression, and their stories are in this book. They often believed that life is just supposed to be miserable. Too often, people accepted being despondent or melancholy as a way of life. As a result, they were held hostage to a life of sadness. Depression completely immobilized them, and they accepted that life could not get better. The very nature of depression created barriers to taking the necessary steps to get better.

To move forward, start by recognizing what depression really is. If what you are experiencing is limiting your life, then you need to take some action. This often requires that you do something new. It can be incredibly difficult to take new action when you have fallen into a pattern of ignoring, concealing, denying, or just living with your sadness.

When depression takes over, doing anything at all is challenging. Change creates unease and is unsettling because we find comfort in the familiar. It feels safer to stick with old habits, making it easy to slip back into doing nothing. Yet if you choose to do nothing, suffering and unhappiness will continue to invade and take over your life.

With this book, my goal has been to provide you enough information so that you can choose what you will be able to do. In order to save yourself from the grip of depression, you need to remember what it means to embrace the good, refrain from the toxic, and enjoy the waves. Those three self-statements are meant to serve as mental buoys to prevent you from sinking further into depression and, instead, guide you to the surface. When you need some more support, there are different types of mental health professionals and a variety of treatment options for you consider.

It is my hope that by understanding depression and the actions you can take against it, you will carve a new path for yourself. This is not about making a new "to-do" list and seeing how many boxes you can check off as completed. This is about taking life one step at a time and rediscovering yourself. This is a call to action for your body, mind, and spirit.

ACKNOWLEDGMENTS

My dear friend Bill Bogan once said that in order to write a book, a book has to be in a person. This book was in me. It was written during the first 12 weeks of the COVID-19 lockdown in Washington, DC as I witnessed the emotional turmoil of those around me.

Although some were technologically prepared to work remotely, it was obvious that the upheaval in our lives was taking an emotional toll on many of us. During the toughest of times my loving husband Mark was always finding new ways to bring me laughter even in the middle of a pandemic. Diego, part of our extended family, left New York City and came to live with us for 13 weeks and brought his joyful exuberance to our lockdown days. Like everyone else we settled into a new pattern for our daily lives. Writing this book filled my new non-commuting hours and late nights.

The urgency to finish this book and get it to people was palpable. On a very fast track Keith Hollaman was once again my editor, Jade K. Meyer provided insightful feedback and edits, Dr. Phyllis R. Freeman (Professor Emerita, SUNY New Paltz, and Senior Researcher, Hudson Valley Healing Arts Center, Hyde

Park, NY) offered extensive comments, and Adolph Falcón as always was enormously insightful and encouraging along the way.

The reality is that this book as well as everything I do would not be possible without the love and support of the people who define my life. My mother Lucy Delgado taught me that the most important acts are those that you do for others. She inspires everything that I am and whatever I do. A day does not go by when I don't hear her words of encouragement.

To help bring this book to life I relied as always on the love of my extended family (Adolph, Bill, Cynthia, Esther, Ileana, Juan, Kevin, Larry, Marti, Priscilla, Roy, and Tomasito); those that add their unique lives and emotional richness to my life (Amanda, who is a reminder that no matter what happens, life is good; Gail, who is an inspiration in more ways than one could imagine; George, with the many nuances of his life; Gladys, who gives me hope for the future; Hanmin and Jennifer, who live what is truly important; and, Sheila and Myrna, who evidence that love is the key to a happy life); and, those who for decades have been a part of my life (Carolina, Diane, Erhard, Laurie, Lourdes, Myra, Polly, Steinar, and Sylvia). And of course, there are the very special people who live forever in my heart: Deborah R. Helvarg, Robert J. Presbie, Margaret M. Heckler, Henrietta Villaescusa, and Msgr. Thomas M. Duffy.

I also want to thank the dedicated board and the fabulous staff of the National Alliance for Hispanic Health and the Healthy Americas Foundation for their support and commitment to the work that we do.

All of these people and many more made this book possible . . . and because of all of our efforts the work will continue. My deepest thanks and gratitude to all.

ENDNOTES

1   Fitzpatrick, KM; Harris, C; and Drawve, G, "Fear of COVID-19 and the mental health consequences in America," *Psychological Trauma: Theory, Research, Practice, and Policy* (2020), advance online publication, https://doi.org/10.1037/tra0000924.

2   Neria Y; Nandi A; and Galea S, "Post-traumatic stress disorder following disasters: a systematic review," *Psychology Medicine* 38, no. 4 (2008): 467–480, doi:10.1017/S0033291707001353.

3   Preston, SD, "The rewarding nature of social contact," *Science*, 357, no. 6358 (September 29, 2017): 1353-54.

4   Nuñez, A; González, P; Talavera, GA; Sanchez-Johnsen, L; Roesch, SC; Davis, SM; Arguelles, W; Womack, VY; Ostrovsky, NW; Ojeda, L; Penedo, FJ; and Gallo, LC, "Machismo, marianismo, and negative cognitive-emotional factors: Findings from the Hispanic Community Health Study/Study of Latinos Sociocultural Ancillary Study," *Journal of Latina/o Psychology* 4, no. 4 (2016): 202–217, https://doi.org/10.1037/lat0000050.

5   Eghaneyan, BH and Murphy, ER, "Measuring mental illness stigma among Hispanics: A systematic review," *Stigma and Health* (2019), advance online publication. https://doi.org/10.1037/sah0000207.

6   Pratt, LA and Brody, DJ, "Depression in the U.S. Household Population, 2009–2012," *NCHS Data Brief*, no.172 (December 2014).

7   Peterson, S and Seligman, MEP, *Character Strengths and Virtues: A Handbook and Classification* (New York: Oxford University Press, 2004).

8   "Depression," National Institute of Mental Health, https://www.nimh.
     nih.gov/health/topics/depression/index.shtml.

9   World Health Organization, Classifications, "ICD purpose and uses."
     https://www.who.int/classifications/icd/en/.

10   Proposal Approved by the DSM Steering Committee, American
     Psychiatric Association, (April 6, 2020) https://www.psychiatry.org/
     psychiatrists/practice/dsm/proposed-changes.

11   Egede LE; Bishu KG; Walker RJ; and Dismuke CE, "Impact of
     diagnosed depression on healthcare costs in adults with and without
     diabetes: United States, 2004–2011," *Journal of Affective Disorders*, 195
     (2016): 119–126, doi: 10.1016/j.jad.2016.02.011.

12   World Health Organization, "Depression and other common mental
     disorders," (2017) WHO/MSD/MER/2017.2.

13   Pratt, LA and Brody, DJ, "Depression in the U.S. Household Population,
     2009–2012," *NCHS Data Brief* no.172 (December 2014).

14   National Institute of Mental Health, "Major depression among adults,"
     www.nimh.nih.gov/health/statistics/prevalence/major-depression-
     among-adults.shtml, accessed July 1, 2016.

15   "Depression," National Institute of Mental Health, https://www.nimh.
     nih.gov/health/topics/depression/index.shtml.

16   Gavin NI; Gaynes, BN; Lohr, KN, Meltzer-Brody, S; Gartlehner, G; and
     Swinson, T, "Perinatal depression: a systematic review of prevalence
     and incidence," *Obstetrics and Gynecology* 106 (2005): 1071–1083, DOI:
     10.1097/01.AOG.0000183597.31630.db.

17   Demyttenaere, K, "What is treatment resistance in psychiatry? A
     'difficult-to-treat' concept," *World Psychiatry* 18, no. 3 (October 2019):
     354–355, published online September 9, 2019, doi: 10.1002/wps.20677.

18   McAllister-Williams, RH; Arango, C; Blier, P; Demyttenaere, K;
     Falkai, P; Gorwood, P; Hopwood, M; Javed, A; Kasper, S; Malhi, GS;
     Soares, JC; Vieta, E; Young, AH; Papadopoulos, A; and Rush, AJ,
     "The identification, assessment and management of difficult-to-treat
     depression: An international consensus statement," *Journal of Affective
     Disorders* 267 (Apr 15, 2020): 264–282, https://doi.org/10.1016/j.
     jad.2020.02.023.

19 DHHS, https://www.hhs.gov/answers/mental-health-and-substance-abuse/does-depression-increase-risk-of-suicide/index.html.

20 Substance Abuse and Mental Health Services Administration, "Key substance use and mental health indicators in the United States: Results from the 2018 National Survey on Drug Use and Health," (2019): HHS Publication No. PEP19-5068, NSDUH Series H-54, Rockville, MD: Center for Behavioral Health Statistics and Quality, Substance Abuse and Mental Health Services Administration, retrieved from https://www. samhsa.gov/data/.

21 Manigault, KA, "The bidirectional relationship between depression and diabetes," *U.S. Pharmacist* 41, no.11 (2016): 26–29, https://www.uspharmacist.com/article/the-bidirectional-relationship-between-depression-and-diabetes.

22 National Heart, Lung, and Blood Institute, "Research Feature: Heart disease and depression: A two-way relationship," (April 16, 2017), https://www.nhlbi.nih.gov/news/2017/heart-disease-and-depression-two-way-relationship.

23 Péquignot, R; Dufouil, C; Prugger, C; Pérés, K; Artero, S; Tzourio, C; and Empana, JP, "High level of depressive symptoms at repeated study visits and risk of coronary heart disease and stroke over 10 years in older adults: The three-city study," *Journal of American Geriatric Society* (January 19, 2016), doi:10.1111/jgs.13872.

24 American Heart Association, "Is Broken Heart Syndrome Real?", https://www.heart.org/en/health-topics/cardiomyopathy/what-is-cardiomyopathy-in-adults/is-broken-heart-syndrome-real.

25 Khandaker, GM; Zuber, V; Rees, JMB; Carvalho, L; Mason, AM; Gkatzionis, A; Jones, PB; and Burgess, S, "Shared mechanisms between coronary heart disease and depression: findings from a large UK general population-based cohort," *Molecular Psychiatry*, published online March 19, 2019, https://doi.org/10.1038/s41380-019-0395-3.

26 Dhar, AK and Barton, DA, "Depression and the link with cardiovascular disease," *Frontiers in Psychiatry* 7, no. 33 (2016), published online March 21, 2016, doi: 10.3389/fpsyt.2016.00033.

27 National Institute of Mental Health "Depression: Signs and Symptoms," https://www.nimh.nih.gov/health/topics/depression/index.shtml.

28 Shadrina, M; Bondarenko, EA; and Slominsky, PA. "Genetic factors in major depression disease," *Frontiers in Psychiatry* (July 23, 2018), https://doi.org/10.3389/fpsyt.2018.00334.

29 K Karg, K; Burmeister, M; and Shedden, K, "The serotonin transporter promoter variant (5-HTTLPR), stress, and depression meta-analysis revisited evidence of genetic moderation," *Archives of General Psychiatry* 68, no. 5 (2011): 444–454, doi:10.1001/archgenpsychiatry.2010.189.

30 Okbay, A; Baselmans, BM; [...]; and Cesarini, D, "Genetic variants associated with subjective well-being, depressive symptoms and neuroticism identified through genome-wide analyses," *Nature Genetics* 48, no. 6 (June 2016): 624–633, published online April 18, 2016, doi: 10.1038/ng.3552.

31 Wray, NR; Ripke, S; [...]; and the Major Depressive Disorder Working Group of the Psychiatric Genomics Consortium, "Genome-wide association analyses identify 44 risk variants and refine the genetic architecture of major depression," *Nature Genetics* 50, no. 5 (2018): 668–681, doi:10.1038/s41588-018-0090-3.

32 Pigoni, A; Delvecchio, G; Altamura, AC; Soares, JC; Fagnani, C; and Brambilla, P, "The role of genes and environment on brain alterations in Major Depressive Disorder: A review of twin studies: Special Section on 'Translational and Neuroscience Studies in Affective Disorders,' section editor, Maria Nobile MD, PhD, *Journal of Affective Disorders* 234 (2018): 346–350, https://doi.org/10.1016/j.jad.2017.10.036.

33 NIH U.S. National Library of Medicine, Genetics Home Reference, "Your Guide to Understanding Genetic Conditions," published June 9, 2020, https://ghr.nlm.nih.gov/condition/depression#inheritance.

34 Bickart, KC; Wright, CI; Dautoff, RJ; Dickerson, BC; and Barrett, LF, "Amygdala volume and social network size in humans," *Nature Neuroscience* 14 (2011): 163–164, https://doi.org/10.1038/nn.2724.

35 Von Der Heide, R; Vyas, G; and Olson, IR, "The social network-network: size is predicted by brain structure and function in the amygdala and paralimbic regions," *Social Cognitive and Affective Neuroscience* 9, no. 12 (December 2014): 1962–1972, https://doi.org/10.1093/scan/nsu009.

36 Möhler, H., "Review: The GABA system in anxiety and depression and its therapeutic potential," *Neuropharmacology* 62, no. 1 (January 2012): 42–53.

37 Acevedo, BP; Aron, A; Fisher, HE; and Brown, LL, "Neural correlates of long-term intense romantic love," *Social Cognitive and Affective Neuroscience* 7, no. 2 (February 2012): 145–159, https://doi.org/10.1093/scan/nsq092.

38 Medline Plus. "Hormones," https://medlineplus.gov/hormones.html.

39 Garland, T; Jr, Zhao, M; and Saltzman, W, "Hormones and the evolution of complex traits: Insights from artificial selection on behavior. *Integrative and comparative biology* 56, no. 2 (2016): 207–224, https://doi.org/10.1093/icb/icw040.

40 McQuaid, RJ; McInnis, OA; Abizaid, A; and Anisman, H, "Making room for oxytocin in understanding depression," *Neuroscience & Biobehavioral Reviews* 45 (September 2014): *305–322.*

41 Pennisi, E, "Meet the Psychobiome," *Science* 368, no. 6491 (May 8, 2020): 570–573.

42 Marshall, M, "Roots of Mental Illness," *Nature* 581 (May 7, 2020):19–21.

43 "Molly or Ecstasy *3,4-methylenedioxy-methamphetamine* (MDMA) is a synthetic drug that alters mood and perception (awareness of surrounding objects and conditions). It is chemically similar to both stimulants and hallucinogens, producing feelings of increased energy, pleasure, emotional warmth, and distorted sensory and time perception. MDMA was initially popular in the nightclub scene and at all-night dance parties ("raves"), but the drug now affects a broader range of people who more commonly call the drug Ecstasy or Molly," Drug Facts MDMA (Ecstasy/Molly)," *National Institute on Drug Abuse,* Updated June 2020 https://www.drugabuse.gov/publications/drugfacts/mdma-ecstasymolly.

44 La Barbera, JD; Izard, CE; Vietze, P; and Parisi, SA, "Four- and six-month-old infants' visual responses to joy, anger, and neutral expressions," *Child Development* 47 (1976): 535–538.

45 Shipley, G. and Casarez, L. The Importance of Emotional Intelligence and Servant Leadership Working in Concert to Promote Social Responsibility. In J. Dron & S. Mishra (Eds.), *Proceedings of E-Learn:*

World Conference on E-Learning in Corporate, Government, Healthcare, and Higher Education (2017): 735-740. Vancouver, British Columbia, Canada: Association for the Advancement of Computing in Education (AACE). Retrieved June 23, 2020 from https://www.learntechlib.org/primary/p/181253/.

46 Drigas, AS and Papoutsi, C, "A new layered model on emotional intelligence," Behavioral Science (Basel) 8, no. 5 (May 2018), published online May 2, 2018, doi:10.3390/bs8050045.

47 *Bitbrain.* March 29, 2019 https://www.bitbrain.com/blog/difference-feelings-emotions.

48 Orth, U; Berking, M; and Burkhardt, S. "Self-conscious emotions and depression: Rumination explains why shame but not guilt is maladaptive," *Personality and Social Psychology Bulletin* 32, no.12 (December 2006): 1608-1619, DOI: 10.1177/0146167206292958.

49 Engert V; Grant JA; and Strauss B, "Psychosocial factors in disease and treatment—A call for the biopsychosocial model," *JAMA Psychiatry*, published online June 3, 2020, doi:10.1001/jamapsychiatry.2020.0364.

50 Rosenthal, SA; Hooley, JM; Montoya, RM; van der Linden, SL and Steshenko, Y, "The Narcissistic Grandiosity Scale: A measure to distinguish narcissistic grandiosity from high self-esteem," *Assessment 27, no. 3* (2020): 487–507, https://doi.org/10.1177/1073191119858410.

51 Sowislo, JF and Orth, U, "Does low self-esteem predict depression and anxiety? A meta-analysis of longitudinal studies," *Psychological Bulletin 139, no.1* (2013): 213–240, https://doi.org/10.1037/a0028931.

52 Bleidorn, W; Arslan, RC; Denissen, JJA; Rentfrow, PJ; Gebauer, JE; Potter, J; and Gosling, SD. "Age and gender differences in self-esteem—A cross-cultural window," *Journal of Personality and Social Psychology 111,* no.3 (2016): 396–410, https://doi.org/10.1037/pspp0000078.

53 Sarubin, N; Goerigk, S; Padberg, F; Übleis, A; Jobst, A; Erfurt, L; Schumann, C; Nadjiri, A; Dewald-Kaufmann, J; Falkai, P; Bühner, M; Naumann, F; and Hilbert, S, "Self-esteem fully mediates positive life events and depressive symptoms in a sample of 173 patients with affective disorders," *Psychology and Psychotherapy: Theory, Research and Practice 93,* no.1 (2020): 21–35, https://doi.org/10.1111/papt.12205.

54 The Treaty of Hidalgo. This treaty, signed on February 2, 1848, ended the war between the United States and Mexico. By its terms, Mexico ceded 55 percent of its territory, including parts of present-day Arizona, California, New Mexico, Texas, Colorado, Nevada, and Utah, to the United States. https://www.ourdocuments.gov/doc.php?flash=false&doc=26.

55 The Spanish-American War. The Spanish-American War of 1898 ended Spain's colonial empire in the Western Hemisphere and secured the position of the United States as a Pacific power. U.S. victory in the war produced a peace treaty that compelled the Spanish to relinquish claims on Cuba, and to cede sovereignty over Guam, Puerto Rico, and the Philippines to the United States. The United States also annexed the independent state of Hawaii during the conflict. Thus, the war enabled the United States to establish its predominance in the Caribbean region and to pursue its strategic and economic interests in Asia, https://history.state.gov/milestones/1866-1898/spanish-american-war.

56 The Louisiana Purchase included the entirety of Louisiana, Missouri, Arkansas, Iowa, North Dakota, South Dakota, Nebraska, and Oklahoma; as well as most of Kansas, Colorado, Wyoming, Montana, and Minnesota, and parts of New Mexico and Texas. https://history.state.gov/milestones/1801-1829/louisiana-purchase.

57 Araña, M. "The long, only sometimes hidden, history of bigotry against Hispanics." *Washington Post* (August 11, 2019): B4.

58 Alcántara, C; Gallo, LC; Wen, J; Dudley, KA; Wallace, DM; Mossavar-Rahmani, Y; Sotres-Alvarez, D; Zee, PC; Ramos, AR; Petrov, ME; Casement, MD; Hall, MH; Redline, S; and Patel, S. R, "Employment status and the association of sociocultural stress with sleep in the Hispanic Community Health Study/Study of Latinos (HCHS/SOL)," *Sleep: Journal of Sleep and Sleep Disorders Research 42*, no. 4 (2019): 1–10, https://doi.org/10.1093/sleep/zsz002.

59 Allan, BA; Dexter, C; Kinsey, R; and Parker S, "Meaningful work and mental health: job satisfaction as a moderator," *Journal of Mental Health* 27, no. 1 (2018): 38-44.

60 El Ghaziri, N and Darwiche, J, "Adult self-esteem and family relationships: A literature review," *Swiss Journal of Psychology 77*, no. 3 (2018): 99–115, https://doi.org/10.1024/1421-0185/a000212.

61 Lui, PP, "Intergenerational cultural conflict, mental health, and educational outcomes among Asian and Latino/a Americans: Qualitative and meta-analytic review," *Psychological Bulletin 141, no.* 2 (2015): 404-446, https://doi.org/10.1037/a0038449.

62 Pham, S; Lui, PP; and Rollock, D, "Intergenerational cultural conflict, assertiveness, and adjustment among Asian Americans," *Asian American Journal of Psychology*, advance online publication (2020), https://doi.org/10.1037/aap0000189.

63 Calzada, EJ and Sales, A, "Depression among Mexican-origin mothers: Exploring the immigrant paradox," *Cultural Diversity and Ethnic Minority Psychology* 25, no. 2 (2019): 288–298.

64 Corona, K; Senft, N; Campos, B; Chen, C; Shiota, M; and Chentsova-Dutton, YE, "Ethnic variation in gratitude and well-being," *Emotion 20, no.* 3 (2020): 518–524, https://doi.org/10.1037/emo0000582.

65 Liu H and Waite, L, "Bad Marriage, Broken Heart? Age and Gender Differences in the Link between Marital Quality and Cardiovascular Risks among Older Adults," *Journal of Health and Social Behavior* 55, no. 4 (December 2014): 403–423, doi:10.1177/0022146514556893.

66 Bonelli,R; Dew, RE; Koenig, HG; Rosmarin, DH; and Vasegh, S. "Religious and spiritual factors in depression: Review and integration of the research. *Depression Research and Treatment Special Issue* (August 5, 2012), Article ID 962860 https://doi.org/10.1155/2012/962860.

67 Steffen, PR; Masters, KS; and Baldwin, S, "What mediates the relationship between religious service attendance and aspects of well-Being?" *Journal of Religion and Health* 56, (2017): 158–170, https://doi.org/10.1007/s10943-016-0203-1.

68 Moreno, O and Cardemil, E; "The role of religious attendance on mental health among Mexican populations: A contribution toward the discussion of the immigrant health paradox," *American Journal of Orthopsychiatry 88*, no 1 (2018): 10–15. https://doi.org/10.1037/ort0000214.

69   Chen, Y; Koh, HK; Kawachi, I; Botticelli, M; and VanderWeele, TJ, "Religious Service Attendance and Deaths Related to Drugs, Alcohol, and Suicide Among US Health Care Professionals," *JAMA Psychiatry,* published online May 6, 2020, doi:10.1001/jamapsychiatry.2020.0175.

70   Hirshkowitz, M; Whiton, K; Albert, SM; […]; and Hillard, PJA. *National Sleep Foundation's sleep time duration recommendations: methodology and results summary. Sleep Health.* 1, no. 1 (March 2015): 40-43, https://doi.org/10.1016/j.sleh.2014.12.010.

71   Levy, KN; Hlay, JK; Johnson, BN; and Witmer, C, "An attachment theoretical perspective on tend-and-befriend stress reactions," *Evolutionary Psychological Science* 5, (2019): 426–439, https://doi.org/10.1007/s40806-019-00197-x.

72   Akbaraly, TN; Brunner, EJ; Ferrie, JE; Marmot, MG; Kivimaki, M; and Singh-Manoux, A, "Dietary pattern and depressive symptoms in middle age," *British Journal of Psychiatry* 195, no. 5 (November 2009): 408-413.

73   Sheridan, MB, "Mexico is running dry after its beer industry is shut down," *Washington Post* (May 9, 2020), https://www.washingtonpost.com/world/the_americas/mexico-coronavirus-beer-coron a-tecate-modelo-dos-equis/2020/05/09/d856dc5a-8eec-11ea-9322-a29e75effc93_story.html.

74   Substance Abuse and Mental Health Services Administration (SAMHSA), 2018 National Survey on Drug Use and Health (NSDUH), Table 2.1B—Tobacco Product and Alcohol Use in Lifetime, Past Year, and Past Month among Persons Aged 12 or Older, by Age Group: Percentages, 2017 and 2018, https://www.samhsa.gov/data/sites/default/files/cbhsq-reports/NSDUHDetailedTabs2018R2/NSDUHDetTabsSect2pe2018.htm#tab2-1b, accessed December 2, 2019.

75   National Institute on Alcohol Abuse and Alcoholism, "Alcohol's Effects on the Body," https://www.niaaa.nih.gov/alcohols-effects-health/alcohols-effects-body.

76   Rock, CA; Thomson, C; Gansler, T, et al., "American Cancer Society guideline for diet and physical activity for cancer prevention," *CA: A*

Cancer Journal for Clinicians, first published June 9, 2020, https://doi.org/10.3322/caac.21591.

77   Bahorik, AL; Leibowitz, A; Sterling, SA; Travis, A; Weisner, C; and Satre DD, "Patterns of marijuana use among psychiatry patients with depression and its impact on recovery," *Journal of Affective Disorders* 213 (2017): 168-171, doi:10.1016/j.jad.2017.02.016.

78   National Institute of Mental Health, "Brain Stimulation Therapies," https://www.nimh.nih.gov/health/topics/brain-stimulation-therapies/brain-stimulation-therapies.shtml.

79   Berry SM; Broglio K; Bunker M; Jayewardene A; Olin B; and Rush AJ, "A patient-level meta-analysis of studies evaluating vagus nerve stimulation therapy for treatment-resistant depression," *Medical Devices* (Auckland, New Zealand) 6 (2013): 17–35, epub March 1, 2013., doi: 10.2147/MDER.S41017.

80   Food and Drug Administration. FDA permits marketing of transcranial magnetic stimulation for treatment of obsessive-compulsive disorder, press release August 17, 2018, https://www.fda.gov/news-events/press-announcements/fda-permits-marketing-transcranial-magnetic-stimulation-treatment-obsessive-compulsive-disorder#:~:text=Transcranial percent20magnetic percent20 stimulation percent20(TMS) percent20is,certain percent20migraine percent20headaches percent20in percent202013.

81   Cretas, E; Brunini, AR; and Lafer, B, "Magnetic Seizure Therapy for Unipolar and Bipolar Depression: A Systematic Review," *Neuro Plasticity Special Issue* (2015), Article ID 521398, htpps//doi.org/10.1155/2015/521398.

82   Fifer, KM; Small, K; Herrera, S; Liu, YD; and Peccoralo, L, "A novel approach to depression care: Efficacy of an adapted interpersonal therapy in a large, urban primary care setting," *Psychiatric Quarterly (2020)*, advance online publication May 24, 2020 https://doi.org/10.1007/s11126-020-09750-5.

83   Dennis, CL; Grigoriadis, S; Zupancic; J; Kiss, A; and Ravitz, P. "Telephone-based nurse-delivered interpersonal psychotherapy for postpartum depression: Nationwide randomised controlled trial," *The*

*British Journal of Psychiatry (2020), a*dvance online publication, https://doi.org/10.1192/bjp.2019.275.

84 Humpston, C; Benedetti, F; Serfaty, M; Markham, S; Hodsoll, J; Young, AH;, and Veale, D, "Chronotherapy for the rapid treatment of depression: A meta-analysis," *Journal of Affective Disorders 261* (2020): 91–102, https://doi.org/10.1016/j.jad.2019.09.078.

85 Thase, ME. "Are SNRIs more effective than SSRIs? A review of the current state of the controversy," *Psychopharmacology Bulletin* 41, no 2 (2008): 58-85.

86 Minkove, Judy F, "Esketamine: A New Approach for Patients with Treatment-Resistant Depression," *Brainwise* (Fall 2019), https://www.hopkinsmedicine.org/news/articles/esketamine-a-new-approach-for-patients-with-treatment-resistant-depression.

87 Dacarett-Galeano, DJ and Diao, XY, "Brexanolone: A Novel Therapeutic in the Treatment of Postpartum Depression," *The American Journal of Psychiatry Residents Journal* 15, no. 2 (December 5, 2019): 2–4, published online, https://doi.org/10.1176/appi.ajp-rj.2019.150201.

88 Treatment and Therapies, National Institute of Mental Health, https://www.nimh.nih.gov/health/topics/depression/index.shtml#part_145399.

89 National Center for Complementary and Integrative Health, "Depression." February 2020.https://www.nccih.nih.gov/health/depression.

90 Gottlieb, L. "The surprising intimacy of online therapy sessions," *Washington Post (*May 19, 2020): A23.

91 Kritz, F. "Televisits may be here to stay for doctors, patients," *Washington Post* (May 19, 2020): E1, E5.

92 "NIMH 2020 Strategic Plan," National Institute of Mental Health, https://www.nimh.nih.gov/about/strategic-planning-reports/index.shtml.

INDEX

A

abusers, 73
acetylcholine, 36
acupuncture, 88
adolescence, 9, 38
aguantar, 2–3
alcohol, 3, 61, 69, 75-77
alcohol abuse, 76, 119
alternative medicine, 88
amygdala, 35, 114
anxiety, xi, xiv, 8, 18, 28, 38, 44, 61, 115–16
APA's Psychologist Locator, 106

B

baby blues, 18
bacteriophage, 39
balance, xviii, 34, 62
    work-life, 62
beer, 75–76
behavioral changes, 33, 68
behavioral epigenetics, 32

bereavement, 9–10
bereavement exclusion, 10
bipolar disorders, 7, 84
boundaries, 73
    healthy, 59, 74
brain, xiv, xvii–xviii, 30, 32, 34–37, 39–40, 65, 68, 73, 77, 82–85, 90, 92
brain chemistry, 67, 83
brain scans, xvii, 36–37
brain stimulation therapy, xix, 82-85
brexanolone, 92, 121
broken heart syndrome, 25

C

CBT, 86-87, 96
Celexa, 92
cells, 30–31, 35, 37, 39, 68, 77
CHD, 24–25, 113
chemical messengers, 36–37
chemicals, xiv, 25, 36, 39, 70, 77

Made in the USA
Columbia, SC
12 August 2020